KW-468-800

PROSE, POEMS AND PARODIES OF
PERCY FRENCH

PERCY FRENCH

PROSE, POEMS AND PARODIES OF PERCY FRENCH

EDITED BY HIS SISTER
MRS. DE BURGH DALY

WITH FOREWORD BY ALFRED PERCEVAL GRAVES

THE TALBOT PRESS, LIMITED
EIGHTY-NINE TALBOT ST., DUBLIN

First printed	...	...	...	1929
Reprinted	...	...	...	1932
Reprinted	...	...	...	1936
Reprinted	...	...	...	1941
Reprinted	...	...	...	1944
Reprinted	...	...	...	1946
Reprinted	...	...	...	1951
Reprinted	...	...	...	1953
Reprinted	...	...	...	1955
Reprinted	...	...	...	1957
Reprinted	...	...	...	1959
Reprinted	...	...	...	1960
Reprinted (with additional matter)				1962
Reprinted	...	...	...	1964
Reprinted	...	...	...	1966

Made in the Republic of Ireland at The Talbot Press, Dublin

To
the many friends of
WILLIAM PERCY FRENCH,
both old and young,
this book is
dedicated

▼

FOREWORD

By Alfred Perceval Graves.

" I WAS born a boy and have remained one ever since," writes Percy French in the all too short sketch of his early days at Cloonyquin, his father's estate in Roscommon, which introduces Mrs. de Burgh Daly's delightful Chronicles and Poems of her brilliant brother. "Friends and relatives," he goes on, "often urge me to grow up and take an interest in politics, whiskey, race meetings, foreign securities, poor rates, options and other things that men talk about, but no—I am still the small boy messing about with a paintbox, or amusing myself with pencil and paper, while fogies of forty determine the Kaiser's next move.

" I had already a small brother and sister to play with, and having an appetite that varied indirectly with my size, I was soon able to hold my own with both of them, and also to chase wild animals through the trackless woods of Cloonyquin. Once I remember the tables were turned and a turkey-cock pursued me up to the hall-door steps. After that I never went out without my bow and arrows."

But if the turkey-cock had been too much for Percy, without " his artillery," as he admits, he characteristically leaves his sister to tell this touching story of his combined courage and humanity.   " One very hot summer a scare of mad dogs spread through the county.   One or two terrible tragedies had occurred, and many people were very nervous about their dogs. One day, as my brother was helping to prepare a cricket-pitch near our house and my sister and I were watching him, a small dog rushed violently up the avenue, pursued by men and boys shouting, " Mad dog! mad dog!" at the top of their voices.   Calling to Percy to follow us, my sister and I rushed into the house as fast as our legs could carry us, and were dismayed on reaching the porch to find that Percy had not followed, but was quietly walking up to the dog, which, now quite exhausted, lay down by the steps.   He kept off its pursuers, bent down to the dog, and untwisted from its tail a long thin briar, which his quick eye had seen was the real cause of its furious yelping and rushing.   He was but a boy at the time, and I do not think many boys would have run such risk out of pure humanity."

He remained through life the same humane, courageous boy, of the type that goes by that name in the Irish countryside where some men are called " boys " to the end of their days.   But he possessed traits of character rare amongst boys of all ages; for whilst he was one of the happy-go-luckiest beings that ever stepped, he possessed a temper that nothing could ruffle, however much he ruffled other people's, which he constantly did by his absolutely un-business-like ways.   He was a very clever lad in many directions, as a story-teller, as a talker, an actor and an artist, and even took so readily to instruction in Euclid that his father, greatly affected by his school-

master's report of the boy's mathematical powers,
determined to make him an engineer. So he sent
him to Windermere College, where my brother
Arnold and I had been entered years before by
my father, because its Headmaster, George Hale
Puckle, a brother mathematician, had written
a well-known work on Conic Sections. There young
French, as my brother and myself had been, was so
poorly grounded, that, like ourselves, he was wisely
withdrawn for further instruction in Ireland. But
his peculiar gifts had begun to assert themselves at
Windermere, for he got his ears boxed for scribbling
on his atlas:

> " O Scaggerack,
>   Why look so black?"
>   So spake the Cattegat.
> " I've got the sack,"
>   Said the Scaggerack,
>   " Because my nose is flat!"

He also " found ' Prep.' a quiet time, when you
could write scurrilous rhymes, and draw caricatures
of the masters." But his early fatal knowledge of
Euclid pursued him to Foyle College, " where an
eminent mathematician, named Johnson, was requested to put in the finishing touch. Poor man, he
did his best, but even if he had been Jack Johnson,
he could not have hammered the root of the matter
into my head. However, he built up a beautiful
superstructure on the flimsiest foundation, and I
passed into T.C.D. with honours."

As a matter of fact, Percy French was so quick-
witted that he picked up enough mathematics to
qualify, though with difficulty, for an engineering de-

gree. But his real bent, in which he took after his father, a good classical scholar, was literary, and had he taken up classics instead of mathematics, he would have been far better prepared for success as a writer of verse and prose Owing to his lack of interest in science he loitered along, preferring to have a good time in Trinity College. To use his own words: " I think taking up the banjo, lawn tennis, and water-colour painting instead of chemistry, geology and the theory of strains, must have retarded my progress a good deal. But eventually I was allowed to take out my C.E. degree. I believe the Board were afraid I should apply for a pension, if I stayed any longer in T.C.D."

After leaving the University he became an apprentice under Mr. Price, Chief Engineer of the Midland Railway Co. of Ireland; but that he did not take his position seriously at first is proved by his making his first public appearance as an entertainer at Punchestown races as a nigger minstrel, while thus employed, in company with Charles Manners, a fellow apprentice, afterwards a well-known professional singer. No wonder, then, that their engineering coach could tell this tale of those two playboys to his class: " I once had two pupils, two promising pupils, d'ye folla? And I took them into the College Park to teach them how to survey; one held one end of the chain and the other the other; one danced and the other sang; one was Charles Manners, the other was Percy French!"

Percy French had, however, been an entertainer in his own family circle, and in the houses of neigh-bours, especially that of the Godleys; indeed Mr. A. D. Godley, the late Public Orator at Oxford claims,

" that Séances, late at night, over the Drominchin
kitchen fire laid the foundations of his greatness. It
was the banjo that he affected in those days,
played up to by Francis (now Brigadier-General)
Godley with the bones, and by me with the tam-
bourine." Percy French was in equal request as an
entertainer in Dublin houses when at T.C.D., and
later on in Cavan, where he took up the position of
engineer to the Board of Works, and as a Surveyor
of Drains came into that close and happy connection
with the farming class in that county, which made
him such a master of Irish country life and character,
and gives such reality to his Irish sketches and songs.

Meantime he was also giving much of his spare
time (and he always found himself in command of
plenty of it) to painting in water-colours. He had
conceived a love for the scenery of the Irish Midlands,
which is unique in its combination of sun-stricken
mist, brown bogland and green pasturage; solitary
trees and scattered clumps of woodland, hilly fore-
grounds and far-off visionary mountains. After
visiting an exhibition of water-colours in Dublin he
said that he ought to be able to draw as well, sent
in six sketches to the next exhibition, and took five
prizes with them. His art work was entirely im-
pressionist, and some of his sketches made with
almost the same lightning rapidity as he afterwards
employed as an entertainer.

Percy French's songs, written under the influences
before described, began to bring him in money, and
especially the " Mountains of Mourne," admirably
arranged by Dr. Collisson, his future colleague as an
entertainer; but his invested cash came to an end
owing to the failure of a distillery into which he put

it, and he then found himself at a loose end, for
the Board of Works reduced its staff, just about the
time the distillery wound up."

He then became editor of " The Jarvey," a weekly
comic paper, and married on the strength of his
income as its editor. His wife, whom he called " the
Ray of Sunshine," was the beautiful daughter of
Mrs. Armitage Moore, of Arnmore, and sister of
Priscilla, Countess Annesley, and they had a happy
year of married life together. But " The Jarvey "
" having gone down with colours flying," he had to
find another source of income as soon as possible.
The successful result was the production at the
Queen's Theatre of " The Knight of the Road," the
first real Irish musical comedy, written along with
Dr. Collisson, and played to packed houses. But
sorrow succeeded success. He lost his " Ray of
Sunshine " on the anniversary of her wedding day
and her baby only survived her a few weeks. Some
years afterwards he married again, and in 1890 re-
moved to London. In the interval his entertainment,
" Dublin Up-to-Date," in which his talents both as
an artist and as a song writer were in brilliant
evidence, went round the country.* And from that
time out his position as an entertainer stood only
second to that of George Grossmith.

A suggestion was once made that the brilliant pair
should collaborate, but was never carried out. They
would have proved incompatible, owing, in his sister's
opinion, to French's want of interest in any matter
of real business. Dr. Collisson was a man much

* See the " Chronicles," pp. 71-72. In this effort most of the
artistic work was done by Mr. Richard Orpen, and he and his
brother Billy (now the famous Sir William Orpen) did lightning
sketches in the intervals.

more of his own happy-go-lucky character, and they
ran most delightfully in double harness, supplementing
one another's talents in a surprising degree. They
toured Canada, the United States and the West
Indies together, and the letters from Percy French to
his wife and children, describing their adventures
abroad are full of descriptive charm and drollery.
As in life so in death he and the little doctor were
not divided, Collisson dying the day after he had
conducted a memorial service to Percy French's
memory.

One is here tempted to compare, or rather to
contrast, the careers and capacities of Samuel Lover
and Percy French. For both showed remarkable
versatility in like directions, that is to say, as song-
writers, artists and entertainers. But while French
yielded in his own easy-going way to his father's
desire that he should be trained as an engineer
instead of as an artist, Lover, who had determined to
become a painter, flatly refused to follow his father's
profession of stockbroking, and was in consequence
turned out of doors by that brutal man of business.

Perhaps such a rough experience would have been
good for French, as it certainly proved good for
Samuel Lover, who re-emerged a sufficiently brisk
young man of business to contrive to be asked to sing
a song of his own at a Dublin banquet given in
honour of Thomas Moore himself, and to earn that
poet's high appreciation of his musical powers.
Lover then made a hit as a miniature painter, but
when photography supplanted that form of art, and
his stories and songs were not bringing him in a

sufficient income, he boldly went, when an elderly man, into the field as an entertainer and had a great success in this country as well as in America.

But French was every bit as indomitable in his own easy-going, zig-zag fashion. For when he lost his job as an engineer he took to comic journalism, as has been related, and when " The Jarvey " collapsed, stepped on to the stage with a successful musical comedy.

I should imagine from what I have heard of them both that Lover was the better actor, singer and reciter, French a readier jester across the footlights, as well as a finer artist. His Irish sketches, two of which I am pioud to possess, and which he scattered broadcast so liberally, have a special quality in them that may make them extremely valuable hereafter, while Lover's miniatures are practically dead. Again, whilst some of Lover's songs, such as " Molly Carew," " The Low-backed Car," and " I'm not myself at all," deserve immortality, others are little in advance of the stage-Irish songs of the previous generation. Moreover, when French meets Lover at story-telling, as in his " First Lord Lieutenant," he quite holds his own. Again, whilst some of Lover's songs do not ring quite true in their sentiment this never can be said of any of Percy French's. In " Galloping Hogan " French has also written a national ballad, stronger than any of Lover's.

I met Percy French off and on when he was a contributor to Arthur à Beckett's (not Horatio Bottomley's) " John Bull," a penny " Punch," of which I was the assistant editor, and he illustrated very characteiistically some " Recollections of Father O'Flynn," contributed by me to that weekly.

Going to his entertainments with my children, when an overworked Inspector of Schools in London, was a delight to one, who, like him, was brought up among the Irish peasantry at a time when there were happy relations between them and the Irish gentry, and I could therefore keenly appreciate the " wonderful way wid' him " when he sang and told stories about them.

Politics he eschewed, though no doubt he often went about with risk to his life in the 'eighties, when the relations between land-owners and tenants were so unhappy. But even had he lived safe through one of the Irish republican raids, he would probably have said, as he did to his wife and children, when the " all clear " signal had been sounded, after one of the worst German air-attacks on London: " Do you know I think that was quite the pleasantest raid we ever had!" That was the undaunted Percy French all over—the lover, reassurer and charmer of children, who died, owing to his determination to carry out an engagement for which he was not equal, after living to give more wholesome joy to his generation than any entertainer of his time.

ALFRED PERCEVAL GRAVES.

CONTENTS

SHORT PLAYS AND DIALOGUES

SONGS AND POEMS

—

COME BACK, PADDY REILLY

The Garden of Eden has vanished they say,
But I know the lie of it still.
Just turn to the left at the bridge of Finea,
And stop when half-way to Cootehill.
'Tis there I will find it, I know sure enough,
When fortune has come to my call.
Oh, the grass it is green around Ballyjamesduff,
And the blue sky is over it all!
And tones that are tender and tones that are gruff
Are whispering over the sea,
" Come back, Paddy Reilly, to Ballyjamesduff,
Come home, Paddy Reilly, to me."

My Mother once told me that when I was born,
The day that I first saw the light,
I looked down the street on that very first morn
And gave a great crow of delight.
Now most new-born babies appear in a huff
And start with a sorrowfull squall,
But I knew I was born in Ballyjamesduff
And that's why I smiled on them all!
The baby's a man now, he's toil-worn and tough,
Still, whispers come over the sea,
" Come back, Paddy Reilly, to Ballyjamesduff,
Come home, Paddy Reilly, to me."

1

The night that we danced by the light o' the moon,
Wid Phil to the fore wid his flute,
When Phil threw his lip over " Come agin soon,"
He'd dance the foot out o' yer boot!
The day that I took long Magee by the scruff,
For slanderin' Rosie Kilrain;
Then marchin' him straight out of Ballyjamesduff,
Assisted him into a drain.
Oh! sweet are me dreams as the dudeen I puff,
Of whisperings over the sea :
" Come back, Paddy Reilly, to Ballyjamesduff,
Come home, Paddy Reilly, to me."

I've loved the young weeman of every land,
That always came easy to me;
Just barrin' the belles of the Blackamore brand,
And the chocolate shapes of Feegee.
But that sort of love is a moonshining stuff,
And never will addle me brain;
For bells will be ringin' in Ballyjamesduff
For me and me Rosie Kilrain.
And all through their glamour, their gas, and their guff,
A whisper comes over the sea :
" Come back, Paddy Reilly, to Ballyjamesduff,
Come home, Paddy Reilly, to me."

THE MOUNTAINS OF MOURNE

Oh, Mary, this London's a wonderful sight,
Wid the people here workin' by day and by
   night:
   They don't sow potatoes, nor barley, nor wheat,
   But there's gangs o' them diggin' for gold in the
      street—
At least, when I axed them, that's what I was told,
So I just took a hand at this diggin' for gold,
   But for all that I found there, I might as well
      be
   Where the Mountains o' Mourne sweep down to
      the sea.

I believe that, when writin', a wish you expressed
As to how the fine ladies in London were dressed.
   Well, if you'll believe me, when axed to a ball,
   They don't wear a top to their dresses at all !
Oh, I've seen them meself, and you could not, in
      thrath,
Say if they were bound for a ball or a bath—
   Don't be startin' them fashions now, Mary Machree,
   Where the Mountains o' Mourne sweep down to the
      sea.

I seen England's King from the top of a 'bus—
I never knew him, though he means to know us:
  And though by the Saxon we once were oppressed,
  Still, I cheered—God forgive me—I cheered w d
    the rest.
And now that he's visited Erin's green shore,
We'll be much better friends than we've been he e-
    tofore,
  When we've got all we want, we're as quiet as
    can be
  Where the Mountains o' Mourne sweep down to the
    sea.

You remember young Peter O'Loughlin, of course—
Well, here he is now at the head o' the Force.
  I met him to-day, I was crossin' the Strand,
  And he stopped the whole street wid wan wave
    of his hand:
And there we stood talking of days that are gone,
While the whole population of London looked on;
  But for all these great powers, he's wishful like
    me,
  To be back where dark Mourne sweeps down to
    the sea.

There's beautiful girls here—oh, never mind!
With beautiful shapes Nature never designed,
  And lovely complexions, all roses and crame,
  But O'Loughlin remarked wid regard to them same:
" That if at those roses you venture to sip,
The colour might all come away on your lip,"
  So I'll wait for the wild rose that's waitin' for me—
  Where the Mountains o' Mourne sweep down to
    the sea.

(By kind permission of Messrs. Pigott & Co., Ltd.)

THE EMIGRANT'S LETTER

DEAR DANNY,

I'm takin' the pen in me hand
To tell you we're just out o' sight o' the land;
   In the grand Allan liner we're sailin' in style,
   But we're sailin' away from the Emerald Isle;
And a long sort o' sigh seemed to rise from us all
As the waves hid the last bit of ould Donegal.
   Och! it's well to be you that is takin' yer tay
   Where they're cuttin' the corn in Creeshla the day.

I spoke to the captain—he won't turn her round,
And if I swum back I'd be apt to be drowned,
   So here I must stay—oh! I've no cause to fret,
   For their dinner was what you might call a banquet.
But though it is ' sumpchus,' I'd swop the whole lot,
For the ould wooden spoon and the stirabout pot;
   And sweet Katty Farrell a-wettin' the tay
   Where they're cuttin' the corn in Creeshla the day!

If Katey is courted by Patsey or Mick,
Put a word in for me with a lump of a stick,
   Don't kill Patsey outright, he has no sort of chance,
   But Mickey's a rogue you might murther at wance;
For Katey might think as the longer she waits
A boy in the hand is worth two in the States:
   And she'll promise to honour, to love and obey
   Some robber that's roamin' round Creeshla the
      day.

Good-bye to you Dan, there's no more to be said,
And I think the salt wather's got into me head,
   For it dreeps from me eyes when I call to me mind,
   The friends and the colleen I'm leavin' behind;

Oh, Danny, she'll wait; whin I bid her good-bye,
There was just the laste taste of a tear in her eye,
  And a break in her voice whin she said " You might stay,
  But plaze God you'll come back to ould Creeshla some day."

(By kind permission of Messrs. Pigott & Co. Ltd.)

PHIL THE FLUTER'S BALL

HAVE you heard of Phil the Fluter, of the town of Ballymuck?
The times were going hard with him, in fact, the man was bruk ',
So he just sent out a notice to his neighbours, one and all,
As how he'd like their company that ev'ning at a ball.
And when writin' out he was careful to suggest to them,
That if they found a hat of his convaniant to the dure,
The more they put in, whenever he requested them,
" The better would the music be for battherin' the flure."

CHORUS

With the toot of the flute,
And the twiddle of the fiddle, O'
Hopping in the middle, like a herrin' on a griddle. O'
Up, down, hands a-rown'
Crossin' to the wall,
Oh ! hadn't we the gaiety at Phil the Fluter's Ball !

There was Misther Denis Dogherty, who kep' " The
    Runnin' Dog ";
There was little crooked Paddy from the Tiraloughett bog :
There were boys from every Barony, and girls from
    every " art,"
And the beautiful Miss Bradys, in a private ass an' cart.
And along with them came bouncing Mrs. Cafferty,
Little Micky Mulligan was also to the fore;
Rose, Suzanne, and Margaret O'Rafferty,
The flower of Ardmagullion, and the Pride of Pethravore.

[Chorus.]

First little Micky Mulligan got up to show them how,
And then the widda' Cafferty steps out and makes her bow.
" I could dance you off your legs," sez she, " as sure as
    you are born,
If ye'll only make the piper play ' the hare was in the corn'."
So, Phil plays up to the best of his ability,
The lady and the gentleman begin to do their share;
Faith, then Mick, it's you that has agility !
Begorra ! Mrs. Cafferty, yer leppin' like a hare !

[Chorus.]

Then Phil the Fluter tipped a wink to little crooked Pat,
" I think it's nearly time," sez he, " for passin' round
    the hat."
So Paddy passed the caubeen round, and looking mighty
    cute,
Sez, " Ye've got to pay the piper when he toothers on
    the flute."
Then all joined in wid the greatest joviality,
Covering the buckle and the shuffle, and the cut;
Jigs were danced, of the very finest quality,
But the Widda bet the company at " handeling the fut."

[Chorus.]

A FAIRY SONG

STAY, silver ray,
Till our airy way we wing
To the shade of the glade
Where the fairies dance and sing:
The mortals are asleep—
They can never understand
That night brings delight,
It is day in Fairyland.

Float, golden note,
From the lute strings all in tune,
Climb, quiv'ring chime,
Up the moonbeams to the moon.
There is music on the river,
There is music on the strand
Night brings delight,
It is day in Fairyland.

Sing while we swing
From the bluebell's lofty crest.
"Hey! Come and play,
Sleepy songbirds in your nest;
The glow-worm lamps are lit,
Come and join our Elfin band,
Night brings delight,
It is day in Fairyland."

Roam thro' the home
Where the little children sleep,
Light in our flight
Where the curly ringlets peep.
Some shining eyes may see us,
But the babies understand,
Night brings delight,
It is day in Fairyland.

From the Operetta "Freda and the Fairies," by Caroline Maude Viscountess
Hawarden.
(By kind permission of Caroline Maude Viscountess Hawarden.)

PEOPLE I DON'T WANT TO MEET

THERE are people who say
It is wrong to be gay
In this workaday world of ours;
They live far apart
From the pleasures of art
Discarding the sweets for the sours.
One would think from their creeds
God gave us the weeds,
And the Devil provided the flowers.

Of course I'm aware,
Earthly joys are a snare,
And the laugh from my lips I should banish,
I ought to throw dust
On my head—but I must
Catch that silvery gleam ere it vanish.
As my colours combine,
What a kingdom is mine!
Though most of my castles are Spanish.

" ACH, I DUNNO ! "

I'M simply surrounded by lovers,
  Since Da made his fortune in land;
They're comin' in crowds like the plovers
  To ax for me hand.
There's clerks and policemen and teachers,
  Some sandy, some black as a crow;
Ma says ye get used to the creatures,
      But, ach, I dunno !

The convent is in a commotion
  To think of me taking a spouse,
And they wonder I hadn't the notion
  Of taking the vows.
'Tis a beautiful life and a quiet,
  And keeps ye from going below,
As a girl I thought I might try it,
      But, ach, I dunno !

I've none but meself to look after,
  An' marriage it fills me with fears,
I think I'd have less of the laughter
  And more of the tears.
I'll not be a slave like me mother,
  With six of us all in a row,
Even one little baby's a bother,
      But, ach, I dunno !

There's a lad that has taken me fancy,
  I know he's a bit of a limb,
And though marriage is terrible chancy,
  I'd—chance it with him.
He's coming to-night—oh—I tingle,
  From the top of me head to me toe,
I'll tell him I'd rather live single,
      But, ach, I dunno !

(By kind permission of Messrs. Pigott & Co., Ltd.)

McBREEN'S HEIFER

McBreen had two daughters, and each one in turn
Was offered in marriage to Jamsey O'Burn.
Now Kitty was pretty but Jane she was plain,
So to make up the differ, McBreen would explain,
He'd give the best heifer he had on the land,
As a sort of a bonus with Jane, understand.
But then Kitty would charrum a bird off a bush,
And that left the lad in a horrid non-plush.

Chorus

Now there's no denyin' Kitty was remarkably pretty,
Tho' I can't say the same for Jane,
But still there's not the differ of the price of a heifer,
Between the pretty and the plain.

Entirely bothered was Jamsey O'Burn,
He thought that he'd give the schoolmaster a turn.
Sez he to wed Kitty is very good fun,
Still a heifer's a heifer when all's said an' done.
A girl she might lose her good looks anyhow,
And a heifer might grow to an elegant cow.
But still there's no price for the stock, d'ye mind,
And Jane has a face that the Divil designed.

Chorus

Now there's no denyin' Kitty was remarkably pretty,
Tho' I can't say the same for Jane,
But still there's not the differ of the price of a heifer,
Between the pretty and the plain.

The schoolmaster said, with a good deal of sinse,
We'll reduce the two girls to shillin's an' pence;
Add the price of the heifer, then Jane, I'll be bound,
Will come out the top by a couple o' pound.
But still I'm forgettin' that down in Glengall,
The stock is just goin' for nothin' at all.
So Jim thought he'd wait till the end of the year,
Till girls might be cheaper or stock might be dear.

CHORUS

But when he came for Kitty, she was married to
    McVittie,
And McBlane had appropriated Jane,
So whether there's the differ of the price of a heifer,
Is a thing that he never could explain.

BALLYMILLIGAN

(The Old Woman Speaks)

BACK to Ballymilligan, it's there that I would be,
Back to Ballymilligan beside the silver sea,
    The wee white houses peeping out to greet the dawn
        o' day,
    The little trawlers creeping out to fish below the
        bay.
Oh! if I had me will again it's there that I would
    be—
Back in Ballymilligan beside the silver sea.

They've paid me passage over—I've a gran'child on me
    knee—
An' I'm living here in clover in the home they've made
    for me.
    But it hasn't got the charm an' it hasn't got the
        view
    Of the little hillside farm that my Danny brought
        me to.
Oh! to feel the thrill again when he was courting me
Back in Ballymilligan beside the silver sea.

I've been in Wanamakers, and in all the mighty stores,
That covers many acres and have forty diff'rent floors,
    But it's down to Katy Ryan I'd be trav'lin' in me
        shoes,
    To do me bit o' buyin' and to hear the neighbours'
        news,
To pay the weeshy bill again, for sugar and for tea—
Back in Ballymilligan beside the silver sea.

No doubt I'd find a change in it, for time goes rollin'
    on,
I fancy I'd feel strange in it, the old companions
    gone;
    But there is one that's sleeping there—the one that
    I love best,
    Some day I may be creeping there to lay me down
        to rest.
An' then the old grey hill again will shelter him and
    me—
Back in Ballymilligan beside the silver sea.

INNISMEELA.

I CAN only see the moonbeams that on Innismeela
     float,
   But if I slept inside the fairies' ring
I could see them sailing, sailing in their little silver
     boat,
   And I'd hear the song the little people sing.
For the Fairy Man has told me how he slumbered
        there one day,
   And woke to find them dancing on the shore,
And still he hears them singing, though 'tis faint
        and far away
   And he's wishing he was with them ever more.

I've seen the Queen of Fairyland! I've heard her
        wondrous song,
   With her to heights of happiness I've flown,
Now I know the days are weary, now I know the
        nights are long,
   For the one I love has left me all alone.
Innismeela! Innismeela! there's a sleep that knows
        no dream,
   And it's in that dreamless slumber I shall be,
For I know that I shall waken by some still celestial
        stream
   And through the golden light she'll come to me.

THE ROAD TO BALLYBAY

" Is this the road to Ballybay?"
    Sez I to Miss Magee;
" You're leavin' it behind you,"
    Sez Maryanne to me.
  So I turned and walked beside her,
    And 'tis only fair to say
  It was very pleasant walkin'
    On the road to Ballybay.

        Ballybay, Ballybay,
        'Twas a dark and winthry day,
          But the sun was surely shinin'
        On the road to Ballybay.

" Is this the road to fame and wealth?"
    Sez I to Miss Magee;
" Ye've got the brains, ye've got the health,"
    Sez Maryanne to me.
" But still I want a comrade
    To praise me an' to blame,
  An' keep me from the traps that's laid
    Upon the road to fame."

        Ballybay, Ballybay,
        No man could go asthray
          With a guide like her beside him
        On the road to Ballybay.

" Is this the road to Paradise?"
  Sez I to Miss Magee;
" I'm thinkin' that it might be,"
  Sez Maryanne to me.
 Oh, I saw the love-light leppin'
  In a pair of roguish eyes,
 An' I knew we two were steppin'
  On the road to Paradise.

        Ballybay, Ballybay,
        The birds are far away;
          But our hearts they sang together,
        On the road to Ballybay.

(By kind permission of the Editor of *The Lady of the House.*)

THE END OF THE HOLIDAY

FOLD up the box, the wind is chill,
  The hills are turning grey,
To-morrow I must pay my bill,
  And speed me far away,—
Back to the world again—but still
  Thank God for such a day!

RAFTING DOWN THE RIO

COME sit beside the fire, old friend,
  And dream that bamboo stems
Have risen up around us
  'Mid flowers that shine like gems.
And we are back in fairyland,
  And thro' the golden haze
We're rafting down the Rio—
  In the old Jamaica days.

Oh! the old Jamaica days!
  Faintly through that leafy maze
Comes the croon of Creole melodies
  As down the stream one strays;
Till the fireflies sparkle round us
  In those darkened water ways,
And we're rafting down the Rio—
  In the old Jamaica days.

In those mighty mountain ranges
  What memories lie hid,
Through the stricken streets of Kingston
  Stalks the ghost of Captain Kidd.
While a phantom Henry Morgan
  Sets Port Royal in a blaze,
As we're rafting down the Rio—
  In the old Jamaica days.

Oh! the old Jamaica days!
  How we used to lie and laze,
And think of people working
  As a curious kind of craze;
Wear and tear of brain and muscle
  How we wondered if it pays,
As we rafted down the Rio—
  In the old Jamaica days.

There's a terror in the tree tops,
  And where the shadows brood,
For the wild cat and the scorpion
  And the snakes are seeking food.
The alligators blink at us,
  From fever-haunted bays,
And the woods knew Devil worship—
  In those old Jamaica days.

Oh! the old Jamaica days!
  When the sun's mid-winter rays
Have failed to pierce the fogs that fill
  Our murky alley ways.
We'll sit beside the fire, old friend,
  And as the embers blaze,
Go rafting down the Rio—
  In the old Jamaica days.

LATER ON

WHEN we're children at our lessons, it is beautiful
    to think
  Of the good time that is coming later on;
When we've done with silly copybooks and horrid
    pens and ink,
  What a lovely time is coming later on!
The rivers of New Zealand, the mountains of Peru,
The watersheds of Europe, and the tribes of
    Timbuctoo,
All the facts without the fancies, all the tiresome and
    true,
  Will be nowhere in that lovely later on.

We'll forget the foolish fables that were written by
    Fontaine,
  In the pleasant time that's coming later on;
At those twelve times twenty tables we will never
    look again,
  In the lazy time that's coming later on.
The date of Magna Charta, the plot they called " the
    Rye,"
The counties that are bounded by the Humber and
    the Wye,
We may not quite forget them, but we mean to have
    a try
  In the lazy time that's coming later on.

Oh, my optimistic hero, there are lessons you must
    learn,
  In the queer time that is coming later on;
And masters and examiners you'll find at every turn,
  In the hard times that are coming later on.
Miss Fortune is a governess who'll teach you many
    things,
A tutor called Experience will moderate your flings,
You'll learn how men make money, and you'll learn
    that it has wings
  In the strange times that are coming later on.

Then you'll meet the radiant vision who is all the world
    to you
  (You'll attend her mother's lectures later on);
You'll learn that what's enough for one is not enough
    for two,
  Nor enough for half-a-dozen later on.
No, the work is never ended, though for holidays you
    crave,
There are pop-guns to be mended for the Robbers in
    the Cave.
You fancy you're the master, but you find that you're
    a slave
  To a curly-headed tyrant later on.

And so through all your lifetime you are longing for
    the day,
  The lovely day that's coming later on;
When pens and ink and copybooks will all be laid
    away,
  And that day is surely coming later on.

For when you're really tired, having done your level
    best,
When the story's nearly ended, and the sun sets in the
    West,
Then you'll lie down very gently, and the weary will
    find rest,
    And I fancy we'll deserve it—later on.
Later on, later on,
Oh the many friends have gone,
Sweet lips that smiled and loving eyes that shone.
    Through the darkness into light,
      One by one they've winged their flight
And perhaps we'll play together—later on.

TO E. R.

For you once heard the fairy bells,
    And saw the little shehogues play,
And knew at last the magic spells
    That lead the lover to Glenveigh.

O Poet, when the touch of Time
    Has turned those auburn locks to grey,
Still may the Bells of Faerie chime,
    That once re-echoed round Glenveigh.

THINGS THAT MATTER

FATHER'S lost all the money he made.
  I think it's the best bit of fun;
He says I must go into trade
  And make bricks, like my gran'papa done.

We're living out here in a wood,
  We don't have no pie and no cake;
But, lordy! the fishes are good
  I help him to catch in the lake!

We were going abroad for a spell,
  A tutor had me in his clutch;
And Sis was to learn how to yell
  In French and Italian and Dutch.

An' Mother says, " Isn't it sad ?
  No knowledge we e'er can implant."
But I'm a lot gladder than glad,
  For I'm learning the things that I want!

There's no grand piano down here—
  How Sis and I hated the thing—
But Sam plays the banjo by ear
  And we're learning to vamp and to sing.

At Christmas Pa hadn't the cash
  For a single mechanical toy—
But as there is nothing to smash
  I'm not called " a mischievous boy ! "

Ma thinks that I miss the small gals
  That looks down on us now with such airs
But squirrels are awful good pals
  And Sam has a parrot that swears.

We've not seen a doctor for weeks;
  Pa looks like a Bowery Tough;
And Ma has got red in her cheeks
  That isn't put on with a puff.

.   .   .   .

There's just one small cloud in our sky—
  I suppose it is wrong to complain—
But Pa says he is going to try
  And make a big fortune again.

We'll live in some horrible town
  Where no one knows how to have fun;
And he will be Millionaire Brown
  And I'll be his prig of a son!

But meanwhile our money is spent;
  We've nothing to get or to give;
On schools we don't spend a red cent,
  But we're learning—we're learning to live.

(By kind permission of the Editors of the *Irish Cyclist* and *Motor News*.)

EILEEN OGE

(or *The Pride of Petravore*)

EILEEN OGE! an' that the darlin's name is,
Through the Barony her features they were famous;
If we loved her who is there to blame us,
For wasn't she the Pride of Petravore?
But her beauty made us all so shy,
Not a man could look her in the eye,
Boys, O boys! sure that's the reason why
We're mournin' for the Pride of Petravore.

CHORUS

Eileen Oge! me heart is growin' grey
Ever since the day you wandered far away;
Eileen Oge! there's good fish in the say,
But there's no one like the Pride of Petravore.

Friday at the fair of Ballintubber,
Eileen met McGrath the cattle jobber,
I'd like to set me mark upon the robber,
For he stole away the Pride of Petravore.
He never seem'd to see the girl at all,
Even when she ogled him underneath her shawl,
Lookin' big and masterful when she was lookin' small,
Most provoking for the Pride of Petravore.

[*Chorus.*]

So it went as it was in the beginning,
Eileen Oge was bent upon the winning;
Big McGrath contentedly was grinning,
Being courted by the Pride of Petravore.

Sez he " I know a girl that could knock you into fits,"
At that Eileen nearly lost her wits,
The upshot of the ruction was that now the robber sits
With his arm around the Pride of Petravore.

[*Chorus.*]

Boys, O boys ! with fate 'tis hard to grapple,
Of my eye 'tis Eileen was the apple,
And now to see her walkin' to the Chapel
Wid the hardest featured man in Petravore.
Now boys this is all I have to say;
When you do your courtin' make no display,
If you want them to run after you just walk the other
        way,
For they're mostly like the Pride of Petravore.

[*Chorus.*]

THE FISHERMAN'S WIFE

WHEN the dusky veil of the night is drawn
    When clouds unfold and flee,
When song birds wake, and a saffron dawn
    Steals over a silver sea.

Then the bark that she loves is spreading its wings
    To speed on its way again,
And she hears the song that her sailor sings
    As she hauls on the anchor chain.

Alone she stands on the sunlit sands
   And watches the rising sail,
   And a clear call floats to the speeding boats
   As she echoes his parting hail.

With anxious eyes she scans the skies
   As the boats glide on and on—
Till over the brink of the ocean they sink
   And the bark that she loves is gone.

And standing there, a little prayer
   Flies after them over the foam,
And she turns away to the toil that day
   Must bring to her cottage home.

And the wavelets fall on the old sea wall
   And beat on the cold grey stones,
Singing the song they have sung so long
   In their musical monotones.

And now and again a low sweet strain
   Floats up to the cliffs above,
For the eyes are bright and the heart is light
   When we work for the one we love.

There's a glow in the West, and it tells that rest
   From the toils of the day is nigh,
And the great sun flings forth its golden wings
   Ere bidding the world good-bye.

Down the golden ways of the sun's last rays
   He comes to her over the foam,
And hand clasps hand on the dark'ning strand
   When the bark that she loves comes home.

NOT LOST BUT GONE BEFORE

ONCE, only once, upon a time,
We heard the bells of faerie chime,
  And through the golden nights and days
  They sang their Elfin roundelays.
The world and we were in our prime
Once, only once, upon a time.

Has Fairyland for ever flown?
—The darkness falls on me alone,
  For on my sweet companion's eyes
  There shines the light of Paradise.
The heights of joy I cannot climb
As we did once upon a time.

Oh, loved one of the far away,
I know that we shall meet some day,
  And once again walk hand in hand
  Through all the realms of Fairyland.
And Heaven's own harps around us chime,
As they did—once upon a time!

" A REACTION "

(The Editor of the *Motor News* does not endorse the sentiments of his
contributors.)

I WANT to find some place on earth
   Where motors are unknown,
Where hydroplane ne'er skims the main,
   Nor aeroplane's been flown.
High on some heather mountain,
   Beside some hidden stream,
From noise and speed for ever freed,
   I'll lay me down and dream.

I'll dream I hear the reapers as they sing among the
   sheaves,
And the woodquest softly cooing 'mid the rustling of
   the leaves.
The wind among the rushes, the rippling of the
   stream,
Will come to me again and be the burthen of my
   dream.

When all the world on hydroplanes !
   Is rushing through the waves,
And sirens wake the echoes
   Of the seal's remotest caves,
When men rise off the waters
   And go whizzing through the air,
Till the frigate bird who followed them,
   Gives up in sheer despair.

I'll dream of summer mornings when the day had just
  begun,
And the ships went slowly sailing up the pathway of
  the sun,
And the mellow tops'l chanty came floating back to
  me
From those dear old " water bruisers " as they drifted
  out to sea.

> When all the world is flying past !
>   In bi- and monoplanes,
> And not a region unexplored
>   From pole to pole remains.
> When they're whizzing past our windows,
>   And round our chimney pots,
> And raining oil and petrol on
>   Our little garden plots.

I'll dream of peaceful evenings when the crows came
  slowly home,
And the bumble bees sang harmonies around the
  honeycomb.
When the flittermice flew silently along the forest
  glade,
And from the vale the nightingale sighed forth its
  serenade.

And now to find that hallowed spot afar from human
  ken,
Where, haply, motor cars are not, nor aeroplaning
  men.
And there upon that distant hill, while stars their
  watches keep,
I'll dream the earth is standing still and everyone's
  asleep.

(By kind permission of the Editors of the *Irish Cyclist* and *Motor News*.)

GEORGE GROSSMITH
(Died March, 1912)

Lay down the pipe and the tabor,
  Set the bell tolling instead,
He is resting at last from his labour
  George Grossmith is dead!

The mirth and the melody blended,
  The laughter that ran with it all!
Ring down the curtain—'tis ended,
  The player can take no recall.

'Twas first as an actor we found you
  Filling the little Savoy
The Prince of the Jesters we crowned you—
  And wasn't your ' Koko ' a joy!

I see you First Lord on the ocean,
  Surrounded by beautiful belles;
I can see you concocting a potion
  As ' Mr. John Wellington Wells.'

I can see you as Bunthorne sounding
  The deeps of æsthetic despair;
I can see you when pirates were hounding
  You home to their poisonous lair.

But though you were quite the Top-liner,
  As many a playbill has shown;

To me you were funnier—finer,
   When " Piano and I " were alone.

How my neighbour would dig all my ribs in,
   And bellow ' Bravo ! ' and ' Encore ! '
When you acted that skit upon Ibsen,
   Or sang of ' The babe on the shore.'

From everything laughter extracting,
   What millions you've made to rejoice
At the biograph's views on your acting,
   The gramophone's gibes at your voice.

The lady and gentleman shopping—
   Irascible folk in the train—
The dentist who finds he's been stopping
   The tooth that had never a pain !

I have laughed at them times without number,
   I know I could laugh at them still;
But the bright brain is dulled in Death's
     slumber,
   The stage is for others to fill.

And who is there now of us mummers,
   To take up the mantle you threw;
Ten minutes we give the new comers
   —We spent the whole evening with you.

Farewell ! my old friend, when we find you
   In garments celestial clad,
We will gather around and remind you
   Of all the gay laughs we have had.

I can fancy the harps ringing sweeter,
—Can fancy the cherubims' glee,
Can picture the smile of St. Peter,
When welcoming good old G. G.

Farewell! you were ever the one light
That beamed like a beacon ahead;
—Ah me! there's a chill in the sunlight,
George Grossmith is dead!

IN THE STUDIO

ONCE more I paint from memory
The hills of Donegal,
And as they rise—ma Gramachree!
In fancy I recall
The fairy song you sang for me
Beside the waterfall.

And when I paint the sparkling tide
That flows by Slievenaree,
I would the boat again might glide
Across the summer sea,
And bring the fairy to my side
Who sang that song for me.

GALLOPING HOGAN

(An incident in the Siege of Limerick)

" THEY have sent for fresh artillery,
      The guns are on their way,
   God help our hapless Limerick
      When dawns another day."
   Thus speaks the gallant Sarsfield,
      As sadly he recalls
   The famine and despair that lurk
      Behind those crumbling walls.

" And yet one blow for freedom—
      One daring midnight ride!
   And William may be humbled yet,
      For all his power and pride!
   " Go! Bring to me ' The Galloper,'
      To Highway Hogan say
   'Tis Ireland has need of him,
      And him alone to-day!"

   The Soldier and the Highwayman
      Are standing face to face,
   The fearless front, the eagle eye,
      In both of them we trace.
" Hogan! the night is dark and drear,
      Say, canst thou lead the way
   To Keeper Mountain's black ravines
      Ere dawn another day?"

" Can the eagle find his eyrie?
    Can the fox forget his den?
I can lead ye as none other
    Of the Slievecamatha men.
The black mare knows it blindfold,
    It's not by the stars she'll steer,
Ye'll be to-night on the Keeper's height—
    And dawn will find ye here.''

" Lead on!'' and well he led them,
    Though the Shannon ford ran deep,
And though the white-lipped flood ran fierce
    Around O'Brien's Keep.
The sentinel on Killaloe
    Looked out, but failed to see—
Five hundred silent horsemen ride
    Behind the Rapparee.

That night by Balleneety's towers
    The English gunners lay.
" King William's Camp and safety lies
    But twelve short miles away.
What need of further caution?
    What Irish wolf would dare
To prowl around our camp to-night,
    So near the lion's lair?''

An Irish wolf is near them now,
    And Irish ears have heard
The chosen watchword for the night,
    And " Sarsfield '' was the word.
A tramp of horse—" Who's there? The word!''
    " Sarsfield!'' the answer ran,
And then the sword smote downwards,
    " Ay, and Sarsfield is the man!''

"To arms! the foe!" Too late, too late,
    Though Villiers' vengeful blade
  Is wet with Hogan's life blood,
    As he leads the ambuscade.
  Then foot to foot, and hand to hand,
    They battle round the guns,
  Till victory declares itself
    For Erin's daring sons.

"Oh for those guns in Limerick now
    Placed on the city walls!
  We'd bid King William breakfast
    On his own black cannon balls!
  It may not be—but trebly charged,
    And filled with shot and shell,
  They'll toll the robber's requiem,
    And sound the soldier's knell."

  Oh, sudden flash of blinding light!
    Oh, hollow-sounding roar!
  Down history's page in Irish ears
    It echoes evermore.
  And Balleneety's blackened tower
    Still marks the famous place
  Where Sarsfield staked his all to win,
    And won that midnight race!

AN IRISH MOTHER

A WEE slip drawin' water,
  Me ould man at the plough,
No grown-up son nor daughter,
  That's the way we're farmin' now.
" No work and little pleasure "
  Was the cry before they wint,
Now they're gettin' both full measure,
  So I ought to be contint.

Great wages men is givin'
  In that land beyant the say,
But 'tis lonely—lonely livin'
  Whin the childher is away.

Och, the baby in the cradle,
  Blue eyes and curlin' hair,
God knows I'd give a gra'dle
  To have little Pether there;
No doubt he'd find it funny
  Lyin' here upon me arm,
Him—that's earnin' the good money,
  On a Californy farm.

Six pounds it was or sivin
  He sint last quarter day,
But 'tis lonely—lonely livin'
  Whin the childher is away.

God is good—none betther,
  And the Divil might be worse,
Each month there comes a letther
  Bringing somethin' for the purse.
And me ould man's heart rejoices
  Whin I read they're doin' fine,
But it's oh! to hear their voices,
  And to feel their hands in mine.

To see the cattle drivin'
  And the young ones makin' hay,
" 'Tis a lonely land to live in
  Whin the childher is away."

Whin the shadders do be fallin'
  On the ould man there an' me,
'Tis hard to keep from callin'
  " Come in, childher, to yer tea!"
I can almost hear them comin'
  Mary, Kate and little Con,—
Och! but I'm the foolish woman,
  Sure they're all grown up an' gone.

That our sins may be forgiven,
  An' not wan go asthray,
I doubt I'd stay in Heaven
  If them childher was away.

THE FOUR FARRELLYS

IN a small hotel in London I was sitting down to dine,
When the waiter brought the register and asked me
    if I'd sign.
And as I signed I saw a name that set my heart
    astir—
A certain " Francis Farrelly" had signed the register.
I knew a lot of Farrellys and out of all the crew
I kept on " sort of wonderin' " which Farrelly were
    you.
And when I'd finished dinner I sat back in my chair,
Going round my native land to find, what Farrelly
    you were.

SOUTH

Were you the keen-eyed Kerryman I met below
    Kenmare,
Who told me that when Ireland fought " the odds
    were never fair."
If Cromwell had met Sarsfield, or met Owen Roe
    O'Neill,
It's not to Misther Gladstone we'd be lookin' for
    repeal.
Would have Ireland for the Irish, not a Saxon to be
    seen,
And only Gaelic spoken in that House in College
    Green.
Told me landlords wor the Divil! their agints ten
    times worse,

And iv'ry sort of government for Ireland was a
  curse!
Oh! if you're that Francis Farrelly, your dreams have
  not come true,
Still, Slainthe! Slainthe! Fransheen! for I like a man
  like you!

NORTH

Or were you the Francis Farrelly that often used to
  say
He'd like to blow them Papishes from Darry walls
  away?
The boy who used to bother me that Orange Lodge
  to join,
And thought that history started with the Battle o'
  the Boyne.—
I was not all with ye, Francis, the Pope is not ma
  friend,
But still I hope, poor man, he'll die without that
  bloody end.—
And when yer quit from care yerself, and get to
  Kingdom Come,
It's no use teachin' you the harp—you'll play the
  Orange drum!
Och! man, ye wor a fighter, of that I had no doubt,
For I seen ye in Belfast one night when the Antrim
  Road was out!
And many a time that evinin' I thought that ye wor
  dead,
The way them Papish pavin' stones was hoppin' off
  yer head.
Oh! if you're the Francis Farrelly who came from
  North Tyrone—
Here's lookin' to ye, Francis, but do leave the Pope
  alone!

EAST

Or were you the Francis Farrelly that in my college
    days

For strolling on the Kingstown Pier had such a curious
    craze ?

D'ye mind them lovely sisters—the blonde and the
    brunette ?

I know I've not forgotten, and I don't think you
    forget !

That picnic at the Dargle—and the other at the
    Scalp—

How my heart was palpitatin'—hers wasn't—not a
    palp !

Someone said ye married money—and maybe ye were
    wise,

But the gold you loved was in her hair, and the
    di'monds in her eyes !

So I like to think ye married her and that you're with
    her yet,

'Twas some " meleesha " officer that married the
    brunette;

But the blonde one always loved ye, and I knew you
    loved her too,

So me blessin's on ye, Francis, and the blue sky over
    you !

WEST

Or were you the Francis Farrelly I met so long ago,

In the bog below Belmullet, in the County of Mayo ?

That long-legged, freckled Francis with the deep-set,
    wistful eyes,

That seemed to take their colour from those ever-
   changing skies,

That put his flute together as I sketched the distant
   scene,

And played me " Planxty Kelly " and the " Wakes of
   Inniskeen."

That told me in the Autumn he'd be sailin' to the
   West

To try and make his fortune and send money to the
   rest.

And would I draw a picture of the place where he
   was born,

And he'd hang it up, and look at it, and not feel so
   forlorn.

And when I had it finished, you got up from where
   you sat,

And you said, " Well, you're the Divil, and I can't
   say more than that."

Oh ! if you're that Francis Farrelly, your fortune may
   be small,

But I'm thinking—thinking—Francis, that I love you
   best of all;

And I never can forget you—though it's years and
   years ago—

In the bog below Belmullet, in the County of Mayo.

TO THE WEST

THE Midland Great Western's doing its best,
  And the circular ticket is safe in my vest;
But I feel that my holiday never begins
  Till I'm in Connemara among the Twelve Pins.

The bank has no fortune of mine to invest
  But there's money enough for the ones I love best;
All the gold that I want I shall find on the whins
  When I'm in Connemara among the Twelve Pins.

Down by the Lough I shall wander once more,
  Where the wavelets lap lap round the stones on the
      shore;
And the mountainy goats will be wagging their chins
  As they pull at the bracken among the Twelve Pins

And it's welcome I'll be, for no longer I'll meet,
  The hard, pallid faces I find in the street;
The girl with blue eyes, and the boy with brown shins,
  Will stand for their pictures among the Twelve
    Pins.

To-night, when all London's with gaslight agleam,
  And the Carlton is filled with Society's cream,
I'll be " takin' me tay " down at ould Johnny Flinn's
  Safe an' away in the heart o' the Pins.

THE KINDLY WELCOME

AH! 'twill only be a shower,
  Tho' the wind is from the West,
Just come in for half-an-hour
  And give yerself a rest.

And was that what ye wor sketchin'—
  Just the turf stack an' the whins?
And yer death o' cowld yer ketchin'—
  Mary Ann, put out them hins!

An' that picture, do ye say now
  Ye could sell for thirty bob?
Still, this paintin' in a way now
  Is a very lonesome job.

.   .   .   .

Oh! now yer welcome, honey,
  To a little sup like that;
Is it me be takin' money
  For what wouldn't feed the cat!

IN EXILE

This London sky is dull and grey;
  A storm of sleet and rain
Is beating dismally to-day
  Upon my window pane.
On wings of fancy let me stray
  To summer shores again.

Once more the fresh Atlantic breeze
  Its friendly greeting cries;
Afar across the azure seas
  The cliffs of Achill rise
And cloudlands countless pageantries
  Sweep thro' the sunlit skies.

The distance fills with misty hills,
  Alternate gleam and gloom;
I see again the purple plain
  Bestarred with golden broom,
Whilst at my feet the meadowsweet
  Pours forth its faint perfume.

So when along the Achill Sound
  The Summer sunset gleams,
And when the heather bells are found,
  Beside the mountain streams,
I'll seek thy shore and live once more,
  Oh island of my dreams!

WHISTLIN' PHIL McHUGH

Oh ! Whistlin' Phil McHugh,
Has come over from Bunlaghy,
An' we don't know what's come to
Little Mary Ann Mulcahy,
For ever since the day
That Phil he came a whistlin',
She stands in the doorway
An' she's waitin' an' she's lishnin'.

CHORUS

Oh ! Mary you're contrary.
Come in and shut the door;
Phil's a rover, sure 'tis over,
And he'll not come back, asthore.
But she's lishnin' for the whistlin'
And she's waitin' by the shore,
For that arrum to be warrum
Round her waist once more.

There's Thady of the Cows,
Sure you know " Ten-acre Thady,"
Wid his fine new slated house
He'd make her quite the lady,
But Thady needn't stay,
And there's no use his inthragin',
For her heart is far away
'Tis wid Phil McHugh stravagin'.

[*Chorus.*]

There's Danny Michael Dan,
Who is six fut in his stockin's,
A very proper man,
But she never heeds his knockin's.
She'll keep him standin' there
For three quarthers of a minit,
But she's racin' like a hare
When she thinks that Phil is in it.

[*Chorus*.]

'Tis wisdom's golden rule
I do teach her till I tire,
That every girl's a fool,
Ay, and every man's a liar.
What's that you say you hear,
That's set you all a thrimbly?
'Tis but the wind, I fear,
That is whistlin' down the chimbly.

CHORUS

Oh! Mary you're contrary,
Come in and bar the door;
What's that scufflin'?
Phil, you ruffian!
Sure I knew he'd come, asthore.
She's been settin' there and frettin'
But now her grievin's o'er;
And the singin' will be ringin'
In her heart once more!

MRS. BRADY

OULD Brady's gone to glory, and the widda has the
    land,
And as she's good to look at, you can easy under-
    stand
That eligible suitors from the town of Athenry
Put on their best embellishments, and thought they'd
    have a try.
Jim Flynn, the stationmaster's son, though not in
    Brady's set,
Was kind enough to say to her, one evening when
    they met:

Chorus:

" Mrs. Brady, just a whisper !
    To your mourning bid adieu !
    I know a fine young gentleman
    Who'd not object to you.
    My family may cut me,
    But you've brass enough for two."
" I know who has the brass," says Mrs. Brady.
" Brass enough for three," says Mrs. Brady.

Pat Dempsey heard that Jimmy had been sent against
    the wall,
Says Pat, " It's not gentility the widda wants at all.
But ' pity is akin to love,' as everybody knows,
I'll tell her how I've got no girl to wash or mend my
    clothes."

He dressed up like a scarecrow that across a field
       was hung,
And this was the comehither that came slipping off
       his tongue:

Chorus:

  " Mrs. Brady, just a whisper!
    I'd be glad to marry you,
    For indeed I've none to help me
    With the work I have to do;
    And the victuals that they cook me
    I can neither chop nor chew."
  " I would not suit the place," says Mrs. Brady,
  " I'd never do the work," says Mrs. Brady.

Then little Francis Fogarty said, " Women, old and
       young,
Have always been deluthered by the civil-spoken
       tongue;
I'll tell her that her cheeks are like the summer rose
       in bloom,
Her eyes are like two diamonds, and her breath is
       sweet perfume,
So off he goes to call on her, all flatthery and lies,
And this was how he started in to carry off his prize:

Chorus:

  " Mrs. Brady, just a whisper!
    There is none as fair as you,
    Your face is like the dawn o' day,
    Your lips are honey dew;
    I'm certain you're an angel,
    And it is from heaven you flew."
  " I believe you're off your head," says Mrs. Brady.
  " You ought to see the vet.," says Mrs. Brady.

When Flynn, who keeps the grocer's shop, and owns
  a bit o' land,
Came home and heard how Pat had got the back of
   Mary's hand,
Says he, " Myself and Mary has been friends through
   thick and thin,
So he put on all his Sunday clothes, and barbarised
   his chin.
He called on her that morning, she was very sweet
   and kind.
And this was how he hinted at the thoughts were in
   his mind:

Chorus:

 " Mrs. Brady, just a whisper!
  Sure I don't know how to woo;
  But I've got a growin' business,
  And I've love enough for two;
  So name the happy day,
  And would to-morrow mornin' do?"
 " Why not this afternoon?" says Mrs. Brady.
 " There's danger in delay!" says Mrs. Brady.

(By kind permission of the Publishers, Joseph Williams, Ltd.)
(Set to music by the late Dr. Houston Collisson.)

RAFFERTY'S RACIN' MARE

YOU'VE not seen Rafferty round this way?
  He's a man with a broken hat,
His tie and his collar are all gone astray
  And his coat for the matter o' that!
We're racin' Rafferty round the place
  Since Rafferty raced his mare,
He's a man with an anxious look on his face
  And a partially murdered air!

Chorus:

    Oh! Rafferty's racin' mare
    We met him at the fair,
    Says he " She'll win, so keep your tin,
    For backin' the racin' mare.
    Oh! Rafferty's racin' mare!
    We thanked him then and there,
    And every lad in Ballinafad
    Went backin' the racin' mare.

I was the jockey they chose to ride—
  And often the owner he sware
That there wasn't a leap in the earth too wide
  To baffle the racin' mare.
Over hurdle and ditch she went like a witch,
  Till she came where the water shone—
I gave her her head, but she stopped at it dead:
  She stopped—and I went on!

Chorus:

Oh! Rafferty's racin' mare
I whirtled through the air
Like a beautiful bird, but never a word
From Rafferty's racin' mare!

"Get up, you lad," says Ballinafad,
    "You'll win the race for us yet."
But I didn't care for the look of the mare,
    Nor the way that her legs were set.
Says they: "The horse'll stay the course,
    She'll stay it—ivery foot."
"You're right," says I—"I don't deny
    She'll stay just where she's put."

Chorus:

Oh! Rafferty's racin' mare!
We danced around her there,
With stones and sticks, and bits o' bricks
We hit her fair and square.
Oh! Rafferty's racin' mare!
The field they leapt it there,
But on the brink she'd stand and—drink,
Would Rafferty's racin' mare.

But where was Rafferty all the time?
    Oh! Rafferty! he's the lad.
There in the ring—he stood like a king,
    Cheerin' the mare like mad.
His brother was there, disguised, of course,
    As a Roosian millionaire;
Giving the odds aginst every horse
    And the longest aginst the mare.

Chorus:

Oh! Rafferty's racin' mare!
'Twas more than we could bear,
When a bookie revealed
He was backin' the field,
Instead of the racin' mare.
We've got the day to spare,
We've got the millionaire;
And we're havin' a race around the place,
And Rafferty—he's the hare!

THE QUEEN'S ADVICE TO LORD ZETLAND BEFORE STARTING FOR IRELAND

(As Overheard and Reported by Larry Flynn, Waiter.)

" SEE here, me Lord," sez she,
" You'll find it hard," sez she,
" To play yer card," sez she,
  " So I'll give ye the tip," sez she,
  " Before ye thrip," sez she.
" Take yer mackintoshes," sez she,
" And yer ould goloshes," sez she,
  " For it's raining there," sez she,
  " If it rains anywhere," sez she.
" You'll be met with ovations," sez she,
" And grand orations," sez she,
  " So have yer reply," sez she,
  " All cut and dhry," sez she.
" Remark out loud," sez she,
" Yer dreadful proud," sez she,
  " At being sent," sez she,
  " To represent," sez she,
" This glorious land," sez she.
" You understand?" sez she.
  " I'm not too clever," sez he,
  " But I'll do me endeavour," sez he.
" Take a party down," sez she,
" To Punchestown," sez she,
  " And give a ball," sez she,
  " In St. Patrick's Hall," sez she;

" Or maybe two," sez she,
" For one mightn't do," sez she,
 " And Merrion Square," sez she,
 " Mightn't care," sez she,
" To be goin' to supper," sez she,
" Wid Baggot Street Upper," sez she.
 " Don't be axin' for ale," sez she,
 " At yer midday male," sez she.
" Make a lot of J.P.'s," sez she,
" 'Tis a cheap way to please," sez she,
 " And sometimes an R.M.," sez she.
 " But not many of them," sez she.
" Then open bazaars," sez she.
" Bless me stars," sez he,
 " That's not much fun," sez he,
 " When all's said and done," sez he.
" Hould on, asthore," sez she,
" There's a thrifle more," sez she,
 " You know, I presume," sez she,
 " At the drawing-room," sez she,
 " There's many a miss," sez she,
 " You'll have to kiss," sez she.
" That's not so bad," sez he.
" Oh, ho! yer a lad!" sez she.
 " I mean for to say," says he,
 " In a fatherly way," sez he.
" Go home, ye ould sinner," sez she,
" I must order me dinner," sez she.
 " Remember and steer," sez she,
 " Uncommonly clear," sez she.
" I know what you mean," sez he,
" Betwixt and between," sez he.
" Up wid the green," sez he,
" And ' God Save the Queen'," sez he.

THE QUEEN'S AFTER-DINNER SPEECH

(As Overheard and Cut into Lengths of Poetry by
  Jamesy Murphy, Deputy-Assistant-Waiter at the
  Viceregal Lodge).

"ME loving subjects," sez she,
"Here's me best respects," sez she,
"An' I'm proud this day," sez she,
"Of the illigant way," sez she,
"Ye gave me the hand," sez she,
"Whin I came to land," sez she.
"There was some people said," sez she,
"They was greatly in dread," sez she,
"I'd be murthered or shot," sez she,
"As like as not," sez she,
"But 'tis mighty clear," sez she,
"'Tis not over here," sez she,
"I have cause to fear," sez she.
"'Tis them Belgiums," sez she,
"That's throwin' bombs," sez she,
"And scarin' the life," sez she,
"Out o' me son and the wife," sez she.
"But in these parts," sez she,
"They have warrum hearts," sez she,
"And they like me well," sez she,
"Barrin' Anna Parnell," sez she.
"I dunno, Earl," sez she,
"What's come to the girl," sez she,
"And that other wan," sez she,

" That Maud Gonne," sez she,
" Dhressin' in black," sez she,
" To welcome me back," sez she;
" Though I don't care," sez she,
" What they wear," sez she,
" An' all that gammon," sez she,
" About me bringin' famine," sez she.
" Now Maud 'ill write," sez she,
" That I brought the blight," sez she,
" Or altered the saysons," sez she,
" For some private raysins," sez she,
" An' I think there's a slate," sez she,
" Off Willie Yeats," sez she.
" He should be at home," sez she,
" French polishin' a pome," sez she,
" An' not writin' letters," sez she,
" About his betters," sez she,
" Paradin' me crimes," sez she,
" In the ' Irish Times '," sez she.
" But what does it matther," sez she,
" This magpie chatther," sez she,
" When that welcomin' roar," sez she,
" Come up from the shore," sez she,
" Right over the foam?" sez she,
" 'Twas like comin' home," sez she,
" An' me heart fairly glowed," sez she,
" Along the Rock Road," sez she,
" An' by Merrion roun'," sez she,
" To Buttherstown," sez she,
" Till I came to the ridge," sez she
" Of the Leeson Street Bridge," sez she,
" An' was welcomed in style," sez she,
" By the beautiful smile," sez she,
" Of me Lord Mayor Pile," sez she.

"(Faith, if I done right," sez she,
" I'd make him a knight," sez she).
" Well, I needn't repeat," sez she,
" How they cheered in each street," sez she,
" Till I came to them lads," sez she,
" Them ' undergrads'," sez she.
" Indeed, an' indeed," sez she,
" I've had many a God-speed," sez she,
" But none to compare," sez she,
" Wid what I got there," sez she.
" Now pass the jug," sez she,
" And fill up each mug," sez she,
" Till I give ye a toast," sez she,
" At which you may boast," sez she.
" I've a power o' sons," sez she,
" All sorts of ones," says she:
" Some quiet as cows," sez she,
" Some always in rows," sez she,
" An' the one gives most trouble," sez she,
" The mother loves double," sez she,
" So drink to the min," sez she,
" That have gone in to win," sez she,
" And are clearin' the way," sez she,
" To Pretoria to-day," sez she.
" In the ' Gap o' Danger'," sez she,
" There's a Connaught Ranger," sez she,
" An' somewhere near," sez she,
" Is a Fusilier," sez she,
" An' the Inniskillings not far," sez she,
" From the Heart o' the War," sez she;
" An' I'll tell you what," sez she,
" They may talk a lot," sez she,
" And them Foreign Baboons," sez she,
" May draw their cartoons," sez she.

" But what they can't draw," sez she,
" Is the Lion's claw," sez she,
" And before our flag's furled," sez she,
" We'll own the wurruld," says she.

GORTNAMONA

LONG, long ago in the woods of Gortnamona,
   I thought the birds were singing in the blackthorn
     tree;
But oh! it was my heart that was ringing, ringing,
     ringing,
   With the joy that you were bringing O my love,
     to me.

Long, long ago, in the woods of Gortnamona,
   I thought the wind was sighing round the black-
     thorn tree;
But oh! it was the banshee that was crying, crying,
     crying,
   And I knew my love was dying far across the sea.

Now if you go through the woods of Gortnamona,
   You hear the raindrops creeping through the black-
     thorn tree.
But oh! it is the tears I am weeping, weeping,
     weeping,
   For the loved one that is sleeping far away from
     me.

SONG OF WILLIAM, INSPECTOR OF DRAINS

LET others betake them to Western Plains
And ease the redman of his ill-gotten gains;
No tomahawk ever shall injure the brains
Of William, the Local Inspector of Drains.

He mounts his tall trap, gives his charger the reins,
And gallops away through the green country lanes,
The Board pays the posting—the balance remains—
With William, the Local Inspector of Drains.

He finds out the holding and what it contains,
Then maps out his system in furlongs and chains
And points out positions for " miners " and
        " mains "—
Such wisdom has William, Inspector of Drains.

He plunges through marshes long haunted by cranes,
Unmindful of how the dark bog-water stains;
Traducers assert that this ardour he feigns,
They little know William, Inspector of Drains!

He stays in his quarters, of course, if it rains,
And wakes the piano's voluptuous strains,
And if of delay the bold tenant complains,
He's sat on by William, Inspector of Drains.

The fair maids of Cavan (this William maintains),
Tho' I think one should take it with salt, a few grains,
Have left in a body their woe-begone swains
For William, the Local Inspector of Drains!

'Tis an onerous post—but the writer refrains
From dwelling at length on its pleasures and pains,
It may not last long, but as yet he remains
                    Yours faithfully,

                              WILLIAM,
                              Inspector of Drains.

THE MARY ANN McHUGH

COME all ye lads who plough the seas and also seize
    the plough,
The cruise of a canal boat I am telling to ye now.
It was the Mary Ann McHugh that braved the angry
    surf
And bore away from Mullingar with a terrible load of
    turf.

And the captain's name was Duff,
His manners they were rough,
    But every cape and headland by its Christian name
    he knew,
And he issued this command—
" Keep her well in sight of land!
    Till we make the port of Dublin in the Mary Ann
    McHugh."

The engine was of one horse-power, propelled wid a
    blackthorn stick,
Wid the wind astarn, and filled with corn, the horse
    went a terrible lick.
We worked her roun' the Hill o' Down, and then
    Kilcock we passed,
And when we seen John Flynn's shebeen, we cried
    out " Land at last."

But the captain, Jamesy Duff,
Cried " Luff! ye lubbers, luff!
   And don't put in near Johnny Flynn
Whatever else ye do.
   Last time we passed his door
   We forgot to pay his score,
So he's got the polis watching for the Mary Ann
      McHugh.

Then up and spake an old sailor who had sailed the
      Irish Sea.
" I pray thee put into yonder port or the crew will
      mutinee;
To put to sea with the boy and me is a cruel thing,
      I think,
With water, water everywhere, and never a drop o'
      drink!"

But the captain, Jamesy Duff,
Said " Enough, my lad, enough!
   No man before the mast shall ever tell me what
      to do.
Clap on all sail at wance,
For that's our only chance,
   To keep from debt and danger in the Mary Ann
      McHugh."

With anxious hearts the vessel starts upon her
      altered course,
The wind and waves they lashed the shore, and the
      pilot lashed the horse,
But all in vain—beneath the strain the rope began to
      part,
And she ran aground on a lump of coal that wasn't
      put down in the chart!

And the captain, Jamesy Duff,
He caught me such a cuff,
   And then he said, " Go heave the lead," while the
      flag at half-mast flew,
But I had had enough
Of the tyrant, Jamesy Duff,
   So I heaved the lead at his head and fled from the
      Mary Anne McHugh.

COME-ALL-YE.

OH! a sailor courted a farmer's daughter;
Who lived contagious to the Isle of Man.
With warbling melodies he did besought her
To marry him before she'd marry any other sort of a
    kind of a man.

But the farmer's daughter had great possessions,
A silver teapot and two pounds in gold;
And says she, '' Would ye marry me, me bould salt
    water sea-sailor,
If I threw them into the ocean cold?''

'' Oh,'' says he, '' I'd marry you, me heart's enchant-
    ment,
If you had nothing but your father's curse!''
So she made up a bundle of all her grand possessions
And threw them into the water . . . . that ends that
    verse.

But the sailor he could swim like a duckling,
So into the water he dived down deep below,
Got hold of the bundle and swam away chuckling.
To think of the times he'd be having when he landed
    down in Ballinasloe.

But the farmer's daughter was kilt with the laughing,
To think of the bundle she'd made up out of a stone . .
Oh! a sailor courted a farmer's daughter,
But now he's wishing that he'd left the girl alone.

PARODIES

THE TENNIS TOURNAMENT: A LAY OF MODERN DUBLIN

(Lord "What-you-may-call-eh?")

THE great Fitzwilliam Tennis Club
　Have met in high conclave,
The Browns and Jones and Robinsons,
　The beautiful and brave.
Now hold they solemn council,
　McConkey in the chair,
In order to determine when
They'll hold their tournament again,
　In green Fitzwilliam Square.

There be thirty bold committee men,
　With bows of green and gold,
Who ever in Fitzwilliam Square
Have made it their peculiar care
　To keep it mown and rolled.
　Morning and eve the thirty
Guarding those courts are seen,
　Traced out aright in lines of white
With Elvery's machine.

65

Gay were the College Races,
  The Lansdowne Sports were gay;
But the great Fitzwilliam Tournament
  Is now our whitest day.
O'er all the lofty hoardings
  And walls which own his sway,
J. Dillon fills with flaming bills
  Anent the coming fray.

J. Dillon and his myrmidons
  Have worked like one o'clock,
And soon, I ween, are posters seen,
  In Booterstown—the Rock—
In Glenageary's wild ravines,
  By Dalkey's lovely bay,
Till ere the morn the bills adorn—
  The sea girt walls of Bray.

This week the only converse is
  Of ball, and bat, and net,
And men hold monster meetings
  To determine what's a "let."
The shopmen, too, have caught the craze,
  And people rush to buy
The "Back-hand-volley" bonnet,
  Or the "Deuce and Vantage" tie.

But now our haughty challenge
  Has reached the Renshaws' home,
Swift, swift the great twin brethren
  Came speeding o'er the foam.
And Lawford and Mulholland
  Have crossed the self-same night,

And marched across the town to where,
All in the great Fitzwilliam Square,
  Was fought the glorious fight.

Oh! brightly shone the sun upon
  The twenty-first of May,
What time the mighty Renshaw rushed,
  All eager, to the fray.
To meet him came the Richardson,
  A Cheshire champion he—
From the green steeps where Mersey leaps
  To join the Irish Sea.

It is not mine to chronicle
  The details of the strife,
How Renshaw hit the ball a whack,
And Chester sent it flying back
  Ere men could mutter "knife."
You'll find it in "The Freeman,"
  Or in the "Irish Times,"
How Renshaw won the final set
And gallant Richardson was 'bet'
(Beaten's the proper word and yet—
  A poet must have rhymes).

Sempronius Attratinus—
  (His other name is Browne),
Is in the great Fitzwilliam Club
  A star of some renown.
A man of mighty muscle,
  A man of iron nerve,
And, when it happens to come off,
  A very deadly serve.

But never had he met before,
  A foe so cool and stern,
And never had he stood against
  The Renshaw's swift return;
Back on the line he drives him,
  And Dublin with dismay
Sees the stout knight in whom they trust
At length recumbent in the dust
  And Renshaw wins the day.

But meanwhile in the " doubles "
  Great deeds of arms were wrought,
Where Gould and Macnamara
  And great Sir Victor fought.
Sir Victor of the long white coat—
  And heather mixture hose,
The courts know well
The " long, stern swell,"
  Who wears such striking clothes.

From far and near the champions fly,
  Undaunted men are they,
To beard the Lion Lawford,
  To break the Renshaw's sway.
They come from lands far distant,
  From countries far away—
A. Rives arrives from Newport,
  And a Coote from Castlerea.
J. Dwight, the small Bostonian,
  Whose ardour never fades,
Garmendier the beautiful—
  And loved of southern maids.

The gallant M. J. Carpendale,
  The Monkstown men prefer;
The Garveys raise the standard high,
  Of Parsonstown—(or Birr).

As sinks the stricken chimney,
  When wind-blasts blow from far,
As falls the money-market,
  When rumour speaks of War;
So sinks, so falls, the Renshaw,
  Beneath the giant stroke
Of him who first was seen to burst
  The great twin-brethren's yoke.

And now when poles are planted,
  And stretched the tennis nets;
When maids are missing volleys,
  And men are serving lets,
With awe and admiration,
  Still is the story told,
How Lawford won the champion cup
  And belt of shining gold.

(From " Lays of Ancient Hens ").

FITZWILLIAM SQUARE

PREFACE

IN the world's great game of tennis
Which from pole to pole is seen,
Let love be the point of starting,
Faults be few and far between;
Raise no wild unseemly racket
From base lines of life break loose,
Win no underhand advantage,
This the moral we deduce.   W. F.

COMRADES, leave me here a little,
Leave me on this classic plain,
Let me in heroic stanzas
Fight the tournament again.
'Tis the place and all around it
As of old the cabmen swear
When colliding at the corners
Leading to Fitzwilliam Square.
Let me hymn those mighty heroes,
Let me sing their deeds sublime,
Let me send their names resounding
Down the ringing grooves of time.
Here let me recall the combat
In a mighty tide of song;
Leave me here and when you want me
Sound upon the dinner gong.

I myself have played at tennis,
Looked upon myself as fair,
Till I saw the world-wide champions
Battling in Fitzwilliam Square :
Then I saw myself a duffer,
Saw that if I longed for fame
I must choose another pastime,
I must seek another game.
Far in some remoter region
Where men play at croquet still,
I will match me with the curate,
I will bend him to my will—
There mid melancholy maidens
I would bear away the palm
Pacing round each wiry crescent
With a meditative calm.
Fool ! again the dream, the fancy,
Fancy 'tis I know full well,
For I hold the tennis duffer
Higher than the croquet swell.
I who once have wielded racquet,
I to join that sorry group,
Pacing on, yet slowly, slowly
Moving on from hoop to hoop.
Not for me the milder pastime,
Tennis is the game I sing,
Better 'tis to fail at tennis
Than to reign a croquet king.
Here upon a bench I pondered
Nourishing this truth sublime
That good play is naught but practice,
And the long result of time.
Many a time I've seen the Renshaws

Rise triumphant from the fray
Like a pair of mighty planets
Shining in the Milky Way:
Often to the white pavilion
Where the sandwiches they munch
Have I seen the lion Lawford
Slowly sloping to his lunch.
In the Spring the city maiden
Comes in latest fashions dressed,
In the Spring the young man's fancy
Gets himself a brighter vest.
And my spirit leaps before me
To behold the coming scene
With the nation's tennis players
Grappling in the central green:
There methinks would be enjoyment
More than city life entails
Than the tramways, than the loopline
Or accelerated mails.
For I dipped into the future,
Far as human eye might see,
Saw the vision of the players
And the tennis that would be:
Saw the steamers filled with champions,
Argosies of mighty males
And the rapid night expresses
Slinking down the coast of Wales.
Far along the Menai Tunnel,
Glare of engine rushing fast,
And the funnels of the " Connaught "
Plunging through the thunderblast;
Till her engines throb no longer,
Gangways to the pier are hurled
And along them pour the coming

Wonders of the tennis world.
Scenting from afar the battle
Comes each never-failing twin,
Comes the swarthy Lawford smiling—
Ever a sardonic grin:
Daring Dwight the " Boston Bantling "
Whom the " Dusky One " they dub,
Comes again to represent her,
Her the " Universal Hub."
See Hibernia's gloomy chieftain,
On his brow the gathering frown,
Innisfallen's sons will cheer thee
In the combat, Ernest Browne.
Chatterton, the lengthy, striding
Through the medley of my dream,
Bears aloft the student-standard
From the groves of Academe.
Chatterton's a lesser Renshaw
And although a champion bold,
Still his back strokes are to Renshaw's
As a cough is to a cold.
In this paradise of pleasure
Where the town and country meet,
Lying like a green Atlantis
In the desert of the street.

  •   •   •   •   •   •   •   •   ▮

Here the cautious poet pauses
Till the great event is o'er,
For it is not well foretelling
What the future has in store:
Whether Renshaw wins or Lawford,

Or Hibernia's stalwart Knight,
Or some unknown meteor flashes
On the world's astonished sight.
Whosoe'er remains the victor,
This the reader will descry,
When the tournament behind him
As a foughten field shall lie.

.   .   .   .

Great Fitzwilliam Square I leave thee,
Basking in the sunset's glow,
For a mighty thirst arises
Tending tea-ward and I go.

HOW HIAWATHA WON THE CUP

IF you ask me, oh, my children
  Whence this legend and tradition,
  Whence this most astounding story,
Whence this tale of tennis playing?
I would answer, I would tell you:
It was written by a poet,
By a poor but pleasant poet,
Who supports an aged landlord,
And a flock of hungry tradesmen,
Not to mention tax collectors,
Gas and water-rate collectors,
Who keep dancing on his doorstep.

So in his suburban attic
He must grind out comic copy!
With his comrade, Hubert Leslie,
Working at the illustrations,
Till their book is on the market,
Selling by the hundred thousand;
Then the vultures are contented
—For the time they are contented—
And the wolves forego their howling
—For a time forego their howling.

When the days were getting longer,
  When the nights were getting shorter,
  In an ocean-going steamer,
Hiawatha came to London;
Came to try our British pastimes;
Spent a week-end up in Scotland
Slaughtering the Capercalzie.
Found the sport was not exciting,
Asked if he might stalk a beater,
Or bring down a brace of bullocks
Who were feeding in the open.
But his host, Sir Angus Bangus,
Said he couldna' jist allow it,
Said it was unpreecedented.

Then the noble Hiawatha
Tried his hand at motor cycling;
Found there was a spice of danger
When you sped beyond the limit.
Killed a dog and maimed a woman,
Telescoped a fat policeman;
But the damage to the cycle
And repairs to the policeman,
Made a hole in his resources;
So he scrapped the motor-cycle.
Then he tried the game of croquet;
Found he could not keep his temper.
Mild-eyed men and mildewed maidens
Used his ball for their advancement,
Used his ball, then left it stranded,
Just behind some wiry crescent,
While he sat and watched them winning,
Sat and plotted their destruction.

Then the noble Hiawatha
  Bought some clubs and started golfing,
  Bought a dozen balls and lost 'em,
Bought them back a little later
From the keen-eyed caddie master;
Broke a club and started swearing,
Using words of awful import,
Till the sympathising caddie
Said, " Oh! man, ye've got the language!
All yer wantin' now is practice!"
But the much disgruntled golfer
Said " The game is too expensive;
Strange that it should come from Scotland."

Then, at last, he tried lawn tennis,
Took to it like duck to water,
Got some tips from drowsy Dixon
(This the tale they tell of Dixon,
How he dreamt that Doust had smacked a
Volley at him in the doubles
And awoke in time to take it!)
Night and day our hero practised,
Till he got so very perfect
That he entered for the singles!
Oh to tell—if space permitted—
How he met the noble " Mavro,"
How he drove him to the base line,
Till the ever graceful Grecian
Lost that look of gay contentment
Often found upon his features.
How he kept McLoughlin busy
Till the " Comet " said, " Say, fellers,
Take me to ma home in 'Frisco.
On the slope, I'm still some pumpkins."

How he made Decugis murmur:
   " Nom d'un nom! c'est un débâcle!"
   Even when he met the holder,
Wilding, the New Zealand wonder;
Even Wilding met his master
In this copper-coloured blizzard,
And succumbed—still grimly smiling
To the skill of Hiawatha.
Then the war-cry of the Shawnees
Rang out o'er the field of battle:
" Let 'em all come on together!
All the men and women warriors,
Heroes of the past and present.
I will beat them!—I have said it!"
Forth they came! A splendid army:
Mrs. Larcombe, Ladies' Champion;
Mrs. Hillyard, six times champion;
Mrs. Chambers, five times champion;
Mrs. Sterry, four times champion;
Parke, who brought the cup of Davis
From the sun-browned courts of Sydney;
Thomas, champion of the Chessboard;
Gauntlett, Rahe, the Lowes, the Powells;
Doust, the Cornstalks' stalwart smiter;
Germot, Kleinschroth, and Caridia,
All come striding forth to battle.
Oh, to have old Homer's stylo,
That I might describe the battle:
How they tripped on one another,
How the air was filled with clamour:
" Your ball!" " My ball!" " Take it!" " Leave
    it!"
Never was there such confusion:

Smiting wildly, all together,
Till the noble Hiawatha
Once more was proclaimed the victor!

> This is all, my gentle reader,
>   That the Poet has to tell you;
>   For I hear sweet voices calling,
> " Daddy! Leslie! tea is ready!"
>   And the weary wings of Fancy
>   Fold themselves until to-morrow.
>   So I know not if the Redskin
>   Sought again his Reservation,
>   There to teach the game of tennis
>   To the squaws and the papooses:
>   All I know is—" Tea is ready!"

A COMIC ADVERTISEMENT

THE Painter and the Pianist
Were walking hand-in-hand,
" Suppose we try," the Painter said,
" To give a one night stand,
With me to write the dialogue,
And you to be the band!

" Suppose we gave six Matinées,"
Replied the Pianist,
" And cater for the young and old
In ways they can't resist."
" Do you suppose," the Painter said,
" That we should both be hissed?"

" I doubt it," said the Pianist,
" *I've* always got recalls,
And you have got a pretty wit,
A wit that never palls."
" We'll give a week," the Painter said,
" In Steinway's pillared Halls."

Now don't forget on Boxing Day,
From three to nearly five,
For just a week this merry pair
Will keep the game alive;
So on that day jump on a 'bus
And tell it where to drive.

And if the driver says he's got
  To go to London Wall,
Or Parsons Green or Shepherd's Bush,
  You answer " Not at all,
The only place that people go
  This week is—Steinway Hall!"

EXCELSIOR

THE shades of night had almost fled
As through a Cavan village sped
A youth who bore upon his tric-
Ycle this somewhat strange device—
                              "Excelsior."

The spokes were polished up, each one,
Gleamed as it caught the rising sun,
And flashed with nickle-plated sheen,
The axles of that strange machine—
                              "Excelsior."

"Don't be an ass," the old man cried,
"The Cavan hills are hard to ride,
Take my advice and get a car."
A voice responded from afar—
                              "Excelsior."

"Oh, stay," the maiden said, "and rest.
Of course you know your business best,
But why you toil the live-long day—
I can't conceive, nor why you say—
                              "Excelsior."

"Fair maid," the youth replied, "I would
That I could stay with thee for good.
But ah, my worldly wealth is small,
And so I must obey the call—
                              "Excelsior."

" Begob," 'twas thus the peasant spoke,
" But that's the quarest sort o' yoke.
  I beg your pardon, sir, but might——"
  A voice replied far up the height—
                              " Excelsior."

  What motive urged his flying feet?
  A rendezvous with maiden sweet?
  —Alas, 'tis time that I reveal
  The secret of thy triple wheel—
                              " Excelsior."

  Methinks it was the greed of gain
  Which urged him thus across the plain.
  No rest thy wheels may know the while
  They pay him eighteen pence per mile—
                              " Excelsior."

THE NURSERY RHYMES

(Re-written by W. Percy French, with some assist-
ance from Edgar Allan Poe, Longfellow, Tennyson,
Byron, Omar Khayyám, Bret Harte, Swinburne,
Burns, Aytoun, Kipling, Macaulay, Browning, Words-
worth, Scott and Tom Hood).

(These lines should be declaimed with great gravity
and dramatic intensity to get the proper effect).

EDGAR ALLAN POE'S SUGGESTION FOR JACK AND JILL

LONG ago into the mountains
Where the ever-flowing fountains
Sparkle in the summer sunshine
As they did in days of yore,
Sparkle as in days of yore,
Came fair Jill, the Farmer's daughter,
Came to fetch a pail of water,
And her lover Jack besought her
He might bear the pail she bore,
Bear it now and evermore.
Ere the low reply was spoken
Jack fell down, his head was broken,
And the pail, of toil the token,
Rolled relentlessly before—
Rolled with raucous din before.
Short was Jill's untimely laughter,
For we find her tumbling after,
And on wings of rhyme we waft her
Through the nursery ever more—
Only this, there's nothing more.

SING A SONG O' SIXPENCE

(Amended by Omar Khayyám)

I SING a song of sixpence and a pie,
In which a choir of tuneful blackbirds lie:
And when the pie was opened and they sing,
A dainty dish to greet a monarch's eye.

The King was in his parlour counting gold,
The Queen's fair fingers bread and honey hold,
The maid was in the garden spreading clothes
Meanwhile the blackbird pie is growing cold.

So if the King cares not for pigeon pie
And if the Queen heeds not their tuneful cry,
Come then with old Kyám* to some fair mead
And we'll discuss the dainty thou and I.

LITTLE JACK HORNER

(In the Byronic Style)

—WITHIN a windowed niche of that high Hall
Sat little Johnny Horner; he did hear
His hungry comrades from the playground call,
And when they bade him share his Christmas cheer
He met their plaint with cold derisive sneer,
Then smiled a smile on seeing them so glum,
Which stretched his gaping mouth from ear to ear:
With callous finger and remorseless thumb
He seized and ate the sole remaining plum.

* Khayyám.

OLD MOTHER HUBBARD

(From Professor Aytoun's Point of View)

COME hither, wee Magreegor, lad,
  And stand beside my knee,
I've told thee once of Old King Cole
  And of his fiddlers three.

I've told thee of the fate that met,
  The would-go-wooing frog,
But never have I told thee yet—
  Of Mother Hubbard's dog.

She sought the cupboard for his meal,
  She sought and found it bare,
She little knew the dog could steal
  The bone that once was there.

With simulated grief he rolled
  Upon the cottage floor
And not a quivering eyelid told
  He'd had that bone before.

JACK SPRAT COULD EAT NO FAT

(Done into Lowland Scotch by Rabbie Burns)

YE ken the tale o' guid man Sprat,
Wha couldna eat a bit o' fat,
But then his wife made up for that,
  So 'twas nae matter.

What she could eat Jock wouldna hae
And sae the vittles passed away,
The dog and cat the neighbours say
  Found empty platter.

LITTLE MISS MUFFET

(A Tennysonian Idyll)

COMRADES, leave me on my tuffet,
  Leave me to my curds and whey;
Call me by the name of Muffet
  When 'tis time to go away.

Unobserved he sat beside her,
  Dropping from the linden tree;
He was but a beastly spider,
  And the maiden Muffet she.

In her ear he whispers grimly
  Let me share your curds and whey,
But the maiden, rising primly,
  Left the bowl and fled away.

And the spider fain would follow,
  But he thought the safer rôle,
Was to stay behind and swallow
  All he found within the bowl.

HUMPTY   DUMPTY

(By Bret Harte.   Colloquial style)

So, stranger, you've come
To my store for a chat,
An' yer settin' right plum
On the wall whar he sat!
Who sat?   Why that cuss Humpty Dumpty,
Haven't they told ye o' that?

Made no sort o' fuss,
While he sat on that wall,
But I guess he scart us
When the fool had a fall;
And the way the King sent out his horses
Jes' showed he was someone—that's all.

Yas, they tried hard to git him together,
With putty and tin tacks and glue,
But he'd come to the end of his tether,
What's that you say?—it ain't true!
Why you Pumpkin! You sawed-off assassin!
Why Humpty, you horse-thief! it's you!

TOM HOOD'S VERSION

Take him up tenderly
After his fall,
There let him mend or lie
Low on the wall.

Dropped from security
  Into the dust,
All his white purity
  Gone when he bust.

All the King's Cavalry
  Came to his aid
As on the gravel he
  Sloppily stayed.

Though they may cleverly
  Tend to the slain
Humpty may never lie
  Heart-whole again.

So when we tell of him
  Turn from his fall
Just the white shell of him
  Only recall.

GOOSEY GOOSEY GANDER
(By various Authors)

KIPLING'S VERSION

AND this is the song that the white woman sings,
  When her baby begins to howl;
The song of the goose and its wanderings
  The song of the fate-led fowl.

The song of the chamber of her whom I loved,
  The song of the chamber where—
I met an old reprobate, scented and gloved,
  And hurled him down the stair.

And wherever the Saxon speech is heard,
  By the pig or the polar bear,
We follow the feet of that wandering bird
  As they wobble from stair to stair.

SWINBURNE'S VERSION

OH whither, oh why, and oh wherefore
  Great goose thou art gosling no more,
With none to caress thee nor care for,
  Wilt wander from floor to floor?

Is it upstairs thy Gandership's goal is,
  Or dost thou descend from above?
To where in her Holy of Holies
  Low lieth my love.

Where I met with the man who is hairless
  And holding his left leg in thrall,
Propelled him, all pallid and prayerless,
  From attic to hall.

MACAULAY'S VERSION

'TWAS Goosey Goosey Gander
Had wandered far away,
From the green steeps
Where Anio leaps
In clouds of silver spray.
This week the stately gander sails
Untended on the tide,
This week the yellow gosling finds
No mother by its side.
This week the large-eyed frog may leap
All careless from the foam,
For Goosey Goosey Gander
Has wandered off to Rome.

But in my lady's chamber
Is terror and affright,
For news they bring
Of a fearsome thing
That wanders through the night.
Then spake the boy in buttons
Give me the knife and fork,
And I will assail
The spectre pale,
That wanders through the dark.
The knife and fork they bring him,
He rushes forth to slay,

One wild death cry
And giblet pie
Is cheap in Rome to-day.

LONGFELLOW'S VERSION

IF you ask me whence the story
Whence the tale and the tradition,
Whence the tale of Goosey Gander,
I would answer " Ask a p'liceman,"
Ask the blue bird the policeman
Whither wanders Goosey Gander?
From its home in Nursery Rhymeland,
Till it reach my lady's chamber,
Where it disappears abruptly
And for ever from my story.
For a man becomes the hero,
Who, renouncing his devotions,
Is subjected by the author
To the most outrageous treatment.
—And I could go on for ever
In this very simple metre,
But the reader mightn't like it,
So perhaps I'd better drop it.

LITTLE BOY BLUE

(By Henry Wadsworth Longfellow)

TELL me not in mournful numbers
  That the cow is in the corn,
If it is Boy Blue that slumbers
  Let him wake and blow his horn.

If the cow has left the shadow
  Of the tree where it had lain,
If the sheep is in the meadow,
  Let the echoes wake again.

Cows are real—cows are earnest,
  If he does not chase her now,
He will find ere eve returnest
  All the corn is in the cow!

BAA BAA BLACK SHEEP

(A la Rudyard Kipling)

(AND this is the song of the black sheep,
And the song of the white sheep too,
And the awk and the armadillo
And the crocodile knows its true).

" Have I wool?" said the Baa Baa Black Sheep.
" You ask me have I wool?
  When I yield each year
  To the shepherd's shear
  As much as three bags full."

" Have I wool?" said the Baa Baa Black Sheep.
" Go forth to the frozen zone,
  And my wool they wear
  Where the polar bear
  And the walrus reign alone."

" Have I wool?" said the Baa Baa Black Sheep.
  Examine the sailor's socks,
  Retaining their heat
  Through the driving sleet,
  And the gales of the Equinox."

  (And this is the song of the Black Sheep,
  And the song of the white sheep too,
  And they make up this song
  As they wander along
  And it's not very hard to do).

TAFFY WAS A WELSHMAN

(Re-told by Robert Browning)

" THAT is the bolster, I have hung it where
  You others hang some trophy from the war
Over the mantel—'tis an old story—Care
  To hear the details of it?—Right you are,—

This Taffy was a Welshman and a thief
  The terms are not synonymous, my friend—
He may by now have turned a newer leaf,
  How runs the saw " 'Tis ne'er too late to mend."

The man was hungry, starving—had no food,
  He knew that I had much to eat and drink
And so he came and stole—you know the mood
  The act needs no analysis, I think.

Then mark the sequel—Taffy stole my beef
  And I, who hold the law's delays in dread
Cæteris paribus stalked my Cymric thief
  And stole the bolster from beneath his head.

He never woke, ah there's the master hand
  To rob a larder—that is not so hard.
If you should ever want some robb'ry planned
  And executed—then, Sir—that's my card.''

LITTLE   BO-PEEP

BROWNING'S   VERSION

GONE! while Bo-peep in a day-dream was pondering,
  Gone! where the grasses were green to the eye,
Over the hills and the valleys a-wandering,
  Scent in the clover, and sun in the sky.

Feel no remorse for them—they've not confessed
      any!
  Give them no thought as they wander and wind,
Home they'll return—to return is their destiny—
  Tails all dejectedly hanging behind.

WORDSWORTH'S   VERSION

  I WALKED with her upon the hill,
    Her grief was very deep,
  Her tears were running like a rill,
    For she had lost her sheep.

" What were they like, my gentle maid,
　　Were they some special kind?"
" They all had heads in front," she said,
　　And all had tails behind!

" Their bodies were between the two,
　　Their mouths were full of teeth,
　And—this, perhaps, may prove a clue—
　　Their legs were underneath."

" If they have legs," I cried with joy,
　　" Your tears you may refrain,
　For 'tis their legs they will employ
　　To bring them home again!"

RIDE A COCK HORSE

SIR WALTER SCOTT'S VERSION

" RIDE on," he cried, nor slackened rein,
　　Until above the wooded plain
　He saw the market-cross again
　　That Banbury's burghers made,
　And there to gaze on fair Elaine
　　His wooden horse he stayed.

　In sooth she was a goodly sight,
　　She rode a steed of snowy white,
　With rings her fingers were bedight,
　　With bells upon her toes.
　At every movement, howe'er slight,
　　Soft melodies arose.

" GOOSEY, GOOSEY, GANDER."

Ye tentless, feckless, Drumlie Goose,
That wanders oop and doon the hoose,
Yer keepers maun be kind and croose,
    Ye'd raise ma dander.
For weel y'ken ye've na excuse
    For sich meander,
I doot ye've coom to feast yer eyes
Where yonder bonnie leddy lies,
Yer gladsome een yer wa'fu' sighs,
    The way ye scanned her,—
Yer no a goose or I'm no wise
    Yer a'a gander.

HOW ROLEY POLEY WOULD BE RE-WRITTEN BY R-DY-D K-PL-NG.

The tale is as old as a Simla Hill,
  And yet it is always new,
The tale of the tear-drops that lovers distil
  From the eyes of the women they woo.

He was round, was young Roland, and sturdy of limb,
  Roley Poley they called him in camp,
And the Major's four daughters were nothing to him
  Though they loved him—the red-headed scamp.

He'd ride out with Mary, play tennis with Kate,
  Fair Fanny to fish he'd invite,
And then in the evening sweet Winnie would wait
  For the kiss when he bade her good-night.

Their mother, who knew he'd ten thousand a year,
  Said she looked on him quite as a son,
But when asked his intentions he made it quite clear
  That " By Jove, don't you know,'' he'd got none.

The fish are forgotten, neglected the net,
  The pony is feeling the lash,
And sweet little Winifred's eyelids are wet
  As she dreams of a ruddy moustache.

The tale is as old as a Simla Hill,
  And yet it is always new,
For changing the name of the hero, they still
  Tell the same little tale about you.

MOTHER'S FAIRIES.

When we children are in bed,
  We hear them calling,
Fairies dressed in green and red
  Help with might and main,
Toys that were left behind the sofa,
Left behind the great enormous sofa,
Books that were lying open wide
  Find their shelves again.

CHORUS.

To and fro when twilight shades are falling
  To and fro when falls the pearly dew,
Sweet and low I hear the fairies calling
  Is there any work for little people
    Left for us to do?

There's the sock that baby lost,
  Found in the morning,
And the ball that Freddie tossed
  Into the street.
Bricks that we left down in the airy
Picked up by the busy little fairy,
Placed in their boxes, all in a row—
    Ain't those fairies sweet?

Mother is the fairy queen,
  We must obey her,
Everywhere that she has been,
  All is put right.
She must employ a lot of fairies,
Oh! a lot of busy little fairies,
Who are at her beck and call,
  All through the night.

CHORUS.

To and fro when twilight shades are falling
    To and fro when falls the pearly dew,
Sweet and low I hear the fairies calling
Is there any work for little people,
    Left for us to do?

THE VALLEY OF DUNLOE.

Have the fairies all departed
And left me broken-hearted,
To mourn the little creatures we loved so long ago?
Ah! most of them have vanished,
But there's one that isn't banished
For I met her as I wandered in the Valley of Dunloe.

I had stopped awhile to render
In its glory all the splendour
Of the great sun slowly rising, and the morning mists
aglow,
And the rocks that rose before me,
And the tree tops bending o'er me,
Standing black against the sunshine that was sweeping
down Dunloe.

I put in trees and grasses,
And the summer cloud that passes,
O'er the mountain and its shadow in the valley far
below.
But what chalk could tell the story,
The glamour and the glory,
When those golden gleams had flooded all the Valley
of Dunloe.

My attempt at shade and colour
Grew dirtier and duller
When compared with radiant nature, and I felt inclined
to go—
And bury my endeavour
In the crystal stream for ever,
When I heard a gentle voice say, " 'Tis a picture of
Dunloe."

I turned, and lo ! a maiden
With a market basket laden
Was watching my endeavour
With her bright face all aglow,
I knew she was a fairy
Though she said her name was Mary,
And her father was a farmer in the Valley of Dunloe.

I asked her if she'd let me
Take her portrait, but she met me
With a shake of raven tresses which I knew she meant
    for " no."
Still in spite of her decision
I can draw with some precision,
The maid who met my vision in the Valley of Dunloe.

And now when e'er I render
That valley in its splendour,
I see a form that's slender, and a face with eyes
    aglow,
And instead of drawing airy
Heights, I find I've drawn sweet Mary
As she stood that summer morning in the Valley of
    Dunloe.

LINES WRITTEN IN PRAISE OF
JOAN PHYLLIS FRENCH

A young lady, who by constantly disregarding my
advice and eating more than was good for her has
attained her eleventh year.

I.

Oh! Joan, when first you saw the light you
    caused us much annoy,
For both your parents thought you might as well
    have been a Boy.

II.

We HAD two daughters, each a gem—so thought—
        Oh! was it strange?
We'd had about enough of them
        A Boy would be a change.

III.

But after standing you for ten long years of
        Peace and War
If you were to be born again we'd want you—
        —As you ARE.

DADDY.

LINES IN A SWISS HOTEL (ANY OF THEM).

There's German in the music room,
    There's French upon the stair,
There's English in the Grand Salon,
    There's laughter everywhere.
A bunch from Boston hold their own
    At every sort of noise,
O Switzerland! O Switzerland!
    The land for healthy boys!

" We're off to bob," " We're off to ski,"
    " We'll not be home till late."
" A curling match?—well, after tea—
    This morning I must skate."
" Our trailing party starts at ten!"
    And off to sport one whirls,
O Switzerland! O Switzerland!
    The land for growing girls!

In leafy dells love weaves his spells
   Where southern sunsets glow,
And hand in hand thro' fairyland
   The lovers wander slow.
But hearts can throb on board a " bob,"
   We want no woodland glades.
O Switzerland! O Switzerland!
   The land for men and maids.

Some day, old friend, I'd love to take
   Our families and go
From London to Lucerne—and walk
   Amid the sun and snow,
And see ourselves in joyous elves
   (Our daughters and our sons,)
O Switzerland! O Switzerland!
   The land for weary ones!

" IF I WAS A LADY."

If I was a lady, I'd wear a hat.
That all the street would be lookin' at,
An' I'd have a ladies' maid, d'ye mind,
To lace and button me dress behind.
A dress that was lined with good sateen,
None o' yer bits o' bombazine,
And the girls with envy would grind their teeth,
When they heard it rustling underneath.
If I was a lady—but then I'm not,
This shawl is the dacentest thing I've got.

If I was a lady I'd drive to the play,
An' I'd look through me opera glass and say—
" I've seen this silly revue before,
The leading lady's an awful bore;
Let's all get up when she starts her song,
An' go an' eat cakes in a resterong."
Then a powder puff on me nosé I'd dab,
An' drive off home in a taxi cab,
If I was a lady—but then I'm not,
A pass to the gallery's all I've got.

If I was a lady—a regular swell,
With a hairy boa, an' a silk umbrel',
'Tis me that would walk into Shelbourne's Hotel,
An' order me dinner—" Some pork an' beans,
An' whatever ye've got in them soup turreens,
Both the sweets, an' a hunk o' cheese,
And oh, a bottle o' porter please."
Then I'd call for me bill and setteling it,
I'd give the waiter a threepenny bit,
If I was a lady—but then I'm not,
—My dinner comes out o' the stirabout pot.
Still there's a lot of show and sham,
Maybe I'm safer the way I am.

" IF."

If I should die to-night,
And you should come,
And stand beside me,
Lying cold and dumb,
And, if while standing there,
You whispered low,
" Here's the ten pounds,
You lent me years ago."
I would arise, although they'd laid me flat,
And say, "What's that?"

If I should die to-night,
But rose to count,
With trembling fingers,
That long lost amount.
I might live on;
    But when
You said, " Here's your umbrella
And your fountain pen,"
For one short space
I'd gaze into thy face
    And then
Drop dead again.

THE MUSICIAN TO HIS LOVE.

Sing me no song!   Give me one silent hour!
   Your nerve is strong, but mine's a fragile flower;
Sing when I'm far from here, say in Hong Kong;
   But, if you love me, dear, sing me no song.

When I the prelude played, and bade you sing,
   Oh! the strange noise we made!   The jangling!
White notes I found were wrong, so were the black!
   For you had pitched the song right in the crack!

If you were dumb, and not a single note
   Could ever come from out that rounded throat,
Songs you might spell on finger and on thumb,
   Oh, I could love you well if you were dumb!

If I were deaf, oh! then I'd let you sing
   In C or F, and watch the guests take wing;
I'd let thee shriek and yell above the treble clef,
   That would not break the spell—if I were deaf!

You have no ear—no ear for tune or rhyme,
   And, it is very clear, no sense of time.
Sing to my wealthy aunt, her nerves are strong,
   But, if it's me you want—sing me no song!

"THE KILLYRAN WRACKERS."

Now, this is the story,
  Of the boys who left our village,
Under Kit Magorey—that military man.
  Some they go for glory,
And some they go for pillage,
  And the latter was the motive with the boys of
    Killyran.

But from the field of glory
There came another story,
  And Colonel Kit Magorey
Gave me to understan'
  At Alma, Balaclava, and, of course, at Inkerman
There was nothing like the Wrackers
  From the town of Killyran.
The mob that took the Malakoff, and also the Redan,
Was that crowd from Casey's corner in the town of
    Killyran.

They tell me that Boney
  At Waterloo was winning,
And so he would have, only the Prussians lent a hand,
  Says Boney, " Alone I
Would send the Britons spinning,
But I cannot stand the music of that Blucher's German
    Band!"

But from the field of glory
There came another story,
  And Colonel Kit Magorey
Gave me to understan'

Says Boneyparte " My veterans have done what
    mortals can
But they couldn't face the Wrackers
    From the town of Killyran !
It's not that Sepoy General who spoilt my finest plan,
It's that regiment of ruffians from the town of
    Killyran ! "

They tell me that Great Britain
    Is soon to be UNdone,
In the " Daily Mail " 'tis written
    And so it must be true.
A great big German army comes annihilating London,
While " Bobs " and all his regulars are beaten black
    and blue.

But from the field of glory
Will come another story,
    And Colonel Kit Magorey
Gives me to understan'
No foe will ever face us, if only in the van
Is that mob of malefactors from the town of Killyran.
And if the Kaiser ever tries the flame of war to fan
Berlin will be bombarded by the Boys of Killyran.

BALLINADDY

What's to do in Ballinaddy?
  What's the band for did ye say?
The man that killed Jack Donahue
  Is coming home to-day!
Oh, the boys of Ballinaddy
  May be neither good nor great,
But there's two things we can do here
  We can love, and we can hate!

I should ha' killed the man meself
  Before the girl went wrong,
But then I never thought she'd go
  An' Jack was big and strong;
An' Regan her old sweetheart
  Was the man to interfere
But he was in a sailin' ship
  So how was he to hear?

When Regan came across the say
  To give the girl his name,
When he heard that she was dead,
  And the story of her shame,
He just put down his naggin,
  An' rached out for his hat
Sayin', " Boys, I must be goin',"
  Soft and paceable—like that.

He was back in half-an-hour,
  An', sez he, " I cannot tell
If the little girl's in Hivin,
  But Jack Donahue's in Hell!"

They brought it in manslaughter,
  " Killed by an unchancy blow."
Ah, but there was HATE behind it,
  That the jury didn't know.

Wan year they gave to Regan,
  And now his time is run,
Oh, we've got the bonfires ready,
  From Knocklade to Cushendun,
There's boys from Ballyneety
  An' girls from Ballinthray,
For the man that murthered Donahue !
  Is coming home to-day.

Oh ! the boys of Ballinaddy
  Are no credit to the State,
But there's two things we can do here,
  We can love—and we can hate !

THE ISLANDS OF ARRAN

The Islands of Arran are callin' me
      Over the foam
Treeless and barren they're callin' me
      Callin' me home,
  Home where you wander along the shore,
  Kind to the feet is that sandy floor,
  And voices are calling me evermore
      Callin' me home.

Over the mountains they sing to me
    Sing to me—
This is the message they bring to me
Out on the sunlit sea :
Send us the word, an' the boat we'll steer
Safe as a bird to the Claddagh pier,
Follow yer heart and you'll find it here
    Safe in its home.

Valley an' mountain is calling me
    Calling me home,
Silvery fountain is calling me
    Over the foam,
Isles of the Blest they were called of yore,
Come home and rest by the sandy shore,
Meehaul alanna, we've missed ye sore,
    Won't ye come home ?

A LITTLE GIRL'S PRAYER.

" Dear Lord—Aunt Jane is good I know
  But then her smiles are scanty,
I do want to be good—but oh!
  Not quite so good as Aunty;
I know that I am understood
  So no more for the present,
P.S.—Make all bad people good
  And all good people—pleasant."

SWEET LAVENDER.

From street to street we wandered on
  A sellin' sprigs o' lavender,
But all my love o' life has gone
  Ever since I lost her.
Sometimes an echo sounding clear
  Will mock me as I pass along,
And make me think I still can hear
  Her old time song.

We never had too much to eat,
  Too little it might often be,
But life was wonderfully sweet
  To her and me.
I meant to call her all my own
  As soon as I had saved a pound,
But she is gone, and I'm alone
  Upon my round.

There were no lilies for the maid
　　Who lay so peacefully at rest,
A bit o' lavender I laid
　　Upon her breast.
The parson says she's better so,
　　From care and want for ever free,
But then she didn't want to go!
　　And wot price me?

CREMORNE.

When Vauxhall had vanished and Ranelagh's reign
Was ending its glories as fashion's fair fane,
A goddess arose and allegiance was sworn
By Belle and by Beau to my Lady Cremorne.

The worship of Beauty was not thought a crime,
Well, not in that early Victorian time;
Laughter and song on the breezes were borne,
They lived and they loved in the Halls of Cremorne.

They were gay, they were gallant, they lived and died
　　　hard,
And fortunes were lost on the turn of a card;
Plucking the roses and planting a thorn,
Playing with love 'neath the lights of Cremorne.

The ladies were careless perhaps, but the men
All guarded their honour most carefully then;
You pushed past a roué, his ruffle was torn,
'Twas pistols for two in a field near Cremorne.

Other times other manners, and Chelsea did well
When she closed the resort of the Beau and the Belle;
The light feet are weary, the gay plumes are shorn
That danced 'neath the lamps of my Lady Cremorne.

Can we sit in judgment?   Can anyone say
The follies of London have all passed away?
Sleep, let her sleep, she is weary and worn,
Dust and ashes is all that is left of Cremorne.

" TELL ME, O CAPTAIN."

" Tell me, O Captain come up from the sea,
    Is there no news from the little green island,
  Is there a woman there waiting for me,
    Calling me back to the land that is my land?"

" A woman there was, but 'tis weary she grew,
    Weary of waiting and weary of weeping,
  Why do you blame her not waiting for you,
    You with your soul set on sowing and reaping?"

" I thought she'd be true to the word that she said,
    I saw the salt tears in her eyes when she said it.
  One more good year and my fortune was made,
    Tell me, O Captain who was it she wedded?"

" Death was the suitor she had to obey,
    He's laid her to rest in a grave in Glasnevin,
  She whispered your name, then they bore her away,
    Go on with your harvest—she's happy in
      heaven."

"PARADISE."

Somewhere east of the Euphrates,
  Hidden now from human eyes,
Men tell me that the gate is
  Of an earthly Paradise.

Some scorn the ancient story—
  Vague tales of long ago,
But I have seen the glory—
  I have been there—and I know.

I have found it—I have found it,
  Though now 'tis but a dream,
I know the woods that bound it,
  I know the silver stream.

．　　　．　　　．

Sweet thoughts we two were thinking
  As we wandered hand in hand,
And, as the sun was sinking,
  We found Enchanted Land.

She turned to me and kissed me,
  With love light in her eyes,
Oh, wealth and fame have missed me,
  But I've been in Paradise!

Not east of the Euphrates,
  Nor guarded from above,
Ah, no, the Golden Gate is
  Where Love has answered Love.

And high born hearts and lowly,
    May find these fields and know,
The song serene and holy,
    Our hearts heard long ago.

The shades of night were falling,
    E'en then across her way,
She heard the Angels calling,
    She wept—but might not stay.

So when the shadows hide me,
    And darkness veils mine eyes,
Sweet Spirit, come and guide me,
    Once more to Paradise.

CELESTIAL PAINTING.

When painters leave this world, we grieve
    For the hand that will work no more,
But who can say that they rest alway
    On that still celestial shore?

No! no! they choose from the rainbow hues,
    And winging from Paradise,
They come to paint, now bold, now faint,
    The tones of our sunset skies.

When I see them there I can almost swear
    That grey is from Whistler's brain!
That crimson flush was Turner's brush!
    And the gold is Claude Lorraine!

OFF TO THE WEST INDIES.

Dear ones in my happy home
We are sailing o'er the foam
Anchor tripped and helm a-lee
(Not quite sure what that may be)
For the Caribbean Sea!

Doctor looking rather pale
Prospect of a six-days' sail!
Only fancy, we shall glide,
Where the wild Bahamas ride.

What they ride I never knew,
Will know it in a day or two—
Live on flying fish and fruits,
Empty scorpions from our boots!

Mounted on a trusty steed,
Chase the deadly centipede,
Beard the beetle in his den,
" On a peak of Darien."

Then with faces wreathed in smiles
Turning from the Windward Isles,
Sail across the wobbling main
Till we reach our homes again.

RETROSPECTION.

A boat upon the billow,
A bird upon the wing,
A boy upon a bicycle
Sailing through the Spring.

List'ning in the greenwood
For redskins in the scrub,
Cows—a herd of buffaloes,
The cat—a tiger cub!

The lonely curlew calling
Meant a maiden in despair,
And the rustling of the rabbit
Was the advent of a bear.

.   .   .   .   .

Could I find again the woodlond
Where I loved to lie and dream,
While the dragon flies were dancing
To the rippling of the stream.

I'd give up all the world has brought
And all that it may bring,
To be that merry boy again
Sailing through the Spring.

"THE ONLY WAY OUT OF IT."

Oh, girls! what am I to do,
　Me father declares I must marry
Whoever he buckles me to,
　I know he'll be terrible sarry.

John Flynn has a beautiful place
　Which he'll settle on me—may God bliss
　　him,
But oh! the red nose on his face
　I don't think I ever could kiss him.

Of his riches Pat Hennissy brags
　In satin an' silk he would dress me;
I'd sooner be sittin' in rags
　Than let that ould miser caress me.

Ould Clancy has acres o' land
　A horse and five cows and a dunkey
But the hair on his face an' his hand—
　Ach! ye might as well marry a munkey.

They all have a likin' for me,
　But lovers like them I am dreadin',
There's only one boy that I see
　That makes me think well of a weddin'.

An' he is so shy with his tongue
　Tho' I know with the love he is scorchin'
Oh! why can't he spake while he's young
　An' not wait till he's made all his fortune.

Oh, here he comes over the brae!
  He's lookin' so bowld and undaunted
I think if I met him half-way
  He might think of the words that are wanted

(Runs off, and if encored, returns.)

Oh, girls, I had to come back
  To tell ye what happened down yonder,
I spoke of the men on me track
  And how they get fonder and fonder.

I told him I didn't want wealth
  But that I was perfectly willin'
To marry a boy with the health
  Altho' he had never a shillin'.

He proposed and I didn't refuse,
  He's the boy I can love and can honour;
I'm off to tell mother the news,
  He's gone to find Father O'Connor.

(Second encore.)

Ah! why are ye keepin' me here
  When ye know I'm an eejit to do so?
An' how can I marry me dear
  When I haven't a stitch of a truso?

He'd marry me just in me shawl—
  But that wouldn't suit me, begorra,
So now it's good-bye to yez all,
  Come an' dance at me weddin' to-morra.

                           (*Exit.*)

THE NEXT LANDING OF THE FRENCH

Oh! the French is on the say,
          Says the Shan Van Voght,
He'll be here widout delay,
          Says the Shan Van Voght.
He's been gone for many a day,
By them Saxons led asthray,
Och, sure them's the boys can pay!
          Says the Shan Van Voght.
He has all his latest jokes,
          Says the Shan Van Voght.
And he draws wid lightning strokes,
          Says the Shan Van Voght.
And that song wid quaint refrain,
Of " The Clare Excursion Train."
You will want to hear again
          Says the Shan Van Voght.
How should Irish songs be sung?
          Says the Shan Van Voght.
Will he try the ancient tongue?
          Says the Shan Van Voght.
Oh! the Irish may be grand
But the tongue at his command,
Is the one we understand,
          Says the Shan Van Voght.
Tho' the Green Isle of the West
May have brought him many a jest,
'Tis the land he loves the best!
          Says the Shan Van Voght.

HIAWATHA'S MOTORING.

If you ask me whence this story,
Whence this tale and this tradition
Of that knut called Hiawatha,
And the maiden Minnehaha—
I would answer from my corner
Of the editorial sanctum
Written with the speed of lightning
While the foreman yells for " copy " :

Once, when autumn winds were sighing
Round about the Adirondacks,
Hiawatha and the lovely
Maid he knew as Minnehaha,
Sat by Sarranac's blue waters,
And he murmured, "I have bartered
Skins of skunk and bear and 'possum
At a most prodigious profit,
Advertising "Autumn Sale On,"
" Sable skins at next to nothing "!
" This the chance is of a lifetime "!
" Be in time or you'll regret it "!
But the dinkyest and swankest
Set of sables on the market
I have kept for Minnehaha."

And the lovely Minnehaha
Put her arms around her lover,
Said, " You are a tophole angel ;
But unless we get a motor,
How am I to show my sables?"

" Motors cost a lot of money,"
Said the cautious Hiawatha ;
" Even when you do the driving,
There's the upkeep and the petrol."
" Half the Narragansetts have them,"
Murmured Minnehaha, pouting ;
" Half the Crows and all the Blackfeet,
All the Hurons and Comanchees
Have a runabout or sidecar."
So the helpless Hiawatha
Said that he would see about it.

When the sun shone on the pine stems,
Hiawatha sought the wigwam
Of his friend the Motor Maker
(Known as " Do-you-in-the-eye-ball ") ;
Said : " I want to hire a motor,
Not a three-ply up-to-dater,
Fire-proof, short wind, self-extractor,
But a cross between a dredger
And a low-geared traction engine."
And the ancient Motor Maker
Placed one finger on his nostril,
Said, " I have an old-time patent,
Made by Messrs. Bosse and Bunkum ;
' Crock de luxe,' the others call it.
Once you use, you abuse it."
" Haul it out," said Hiawatha,
" Push it to my place to-morrow."

On the morrow Minnehaha
Heard a honking and a hooting,
Heard a clanging and a clanking,

Saw a curious shape approaching,
Heralded by shouting urchins,
Saw her lover, Hiawatha
Seated in the snorting monster.
" Jump right in," cried Hiawatha,
" This way for the Bottled Blizzard!
Change here for the Potted Earthquake!
Silently she sat beside him,
Looking in her suit of sables
Like a winsome little kitten.
" Let her go!" cried Hiawatha
To old Do-you-in-the-Eye-ball
(Son of Wink-the-other-Eyelid)
Sachem of the Narragansetts.

Buzz! Bang! fizz! and off it started!
With a crash of clanging metal
Such a ride! oh, how describe it!
It would take a founder member
Of the famous club in Pall Mall,
Piling up the misadventures
Of a lifetime spent a-touring,
To record the weird disasters
That befell that motor party—
Some day, when the printer's devil
Barks up from below for copy
I myself may tell the story
Of that devastating journey.
Anyhow, it served its purpose,
For, that night, when Hiawatha
Bid good-bye to Minnehaha,
In his ear she murmured softly,
" Scrap that car, and buy a cart-horse—

Buy a caravan and cart-horse ;
One that walks deliberately
With a mien serene and stately,
Who will stay and dream and dally
With the herbage of the valley,
Who will drift across the mountains,
Pause beside the pleasant fountains,
So my system may recover
From this journey, oh, my lover!"

And the heron, the Shu-shu-gah,
And the moose, old Umkenawis,
And Unkwunk, the prickly porker,
Heard that night the hearty laughter
Of the noble Hiawatha
And old Do-you-in-the-Eyeball,
As they drank the Fire water
In the wigwam of the former.

—Moral? None that I'm aware of.

RED-LETTER DAYS.

I was feeling slightly seedy
When a letter signed " Mecredy,"
Came across the Irish Channel to my home in London
    town ;
And I said in language shoppy,
Here's the Boss a wantin' copy,"
And my forehead corrugated in a formidable frown.
" Ho! Wagtale, wake from slumber!
For I want our Birthday Number

To contain a set of verses from thy venerable pate.
    Send me something reminiscent
    Of the days when first we listened
To thy songs around the campfire and we'll pay a
    special rate."

    It was not the extra rating
    Sent these waves of thought vibrating
Through the years that lie behind me to the pre-
    pneumatic days,
    When I rode a solid tyre,
    And thought myself a flyer
If I beat the Allens' pony in a race to Ballyhaise.

    But I always love to turn
    To the feast of good St. Hearn,
When with racquets on our handlebars we drank that
    day's delights ;
    How well our wheels would travel
    O'er the Ballyheady gravel,
How good those games of tennis ! how grand our
    appetites !

    I have still a fair digestion,
    But could I—it's a question.
Eat plum pudding and play singles with these stalwart
    friends of mine,
    Then home by moonlight fly it?
    No, Jack Hearn!—let others try it,
You and I will fight those battles o'er the walnuts and
    the wine.
    Then the day I went a-wheeling,
    Round the lovely shores of Sheelin,

When the perfume of the Primrose told that spring
   had really come ;
     And I rode my cycle dreaming.
     That Beauty's eyes were beaming,
And I'd find cead mille failte in the halls of old Cross-
   drum!

     Sweet Glenfinlas! I'm your debtor,
     For many a red letter
Must mark the days we cycled by Lough Katrine's
   silver strand.
     Darrynane! thy sunset glory
     I have painted con amore,
When she and I were members of Mecredy's merry
   band.

     " Oh, my Tour-alluring laddie,"
     I am now a white-haired daddy ;
In an easy chair I'm sitting by a comfortable blaze,
     But my thoughts away are winging
     To the laughter and the singing
And the cycle bells a-ringing in those old red-letter
   days!

L'ENVOI.

Only the seabird now its way may wing
   From crested wave to crest,
And great cloud galleons in the azure swing.—
" After life's battle," they are murmuring,
   " There shall be rest."

S M I L E S .

When the cat has finished breakfast,
And is sitting by the fire,
The cat that all the tabby cats
Persistently admire,
When that most unpleasant animal
The dog, is out of doors,
And pussy thinks of how last night
He settled some old scores,
When he thinks about the big black cat
He knocked right off the tiles—
                    —He smiles.

When gesticulating Frenchmen
Tell the masher about France,
How he must see la belle Paree
Whenever he's ze chance,
When Italians talk of Roma,
And the Spaniards talk of Spain,
The Piccadilly Johnny wears
A look of mild disdain—
When they say that there are other towns
Outside the British Isles,
                    He smiles.

When Jack has met wi' Janet
By the burn ahint the brae,
Ye dinna ken where yon is?
For mysen I canna say.
When the merlas are foorhooing,

An' the beasties in the byre,
There's something in the lassie's een
That sets his heart on fire.
When he says, " I'm no unwillin'
If ye would be marrit whiles,"
She smiles.

When the Yankee tells the British Peer
That in the Empire State
In Washington and Boston
They have culture just as great;
They haven't Will P. Shakespeare,
Or J. Milton in their show,
But they've Field, and Whitcomb Riley,
And they've Harriet Beecher Stowe——
He doesn't contradict them,
Oh, no, he never riles.
He smiles.

When the farmer's man on Sunday
Gets a 'air cut and a shave,
When he meets wi' Doll the dairy maid,
And she says, " Do behave."
When he says, " I've got two pound a week,
I've 'ad another rise."
Her fortune is her golden hair
And pair of diamond eyes;
So when she hangs around his neck
And sez, " I love 'e Giles,"
He smiles.

When the summer girl has got her frocks,
And this year's set of curls,
When she finds that she's the lovliest
Among a crowd of girls,

When the first unwary masculine
Has met her downcast eye,
When he cannot see the other girls
As long as she is nigh,
When she ascertains there's not another
Man for miles and miles!
                              She smiles.

When the German Jew financier
Has bought before the jump,
Manipulates the market,
And unloads before the slump,
When he's harvesting his dollars,
And he finds a goodly crop,
When his friends are at the bottom
And Herr Grabstein's at the top,
When he thinks of all those poor young men
Who did not make their piles.
                              He smiles.

When Michael meets wid Mary,
At the back o' the boreen,
An' says, " Ye've stole me heart away
Ye murtherin' shlieveen."
When she tells him to give over,
" Can't ye leave a girl alone."
He crams his hat down on his eyes,
His heart sinks like a stone.—
When she takes him home the longest road,
And sits on all the stiles
                              He smiles.

FIGHTING McGUIRE.

Now, Gibbon has told the story of old,
  Of the Fall of the Roman Empire,
But I would recall the rise an' the fall
  Of a man of the name of McGuire.
He came to our town as a man of renown,
  And peace was, he said, his desire,
Still he'd frequently state what would be the sad fate
  Of the man who molested McGuire.

Well, we all were afraid of this quarrelsome blade,
  An' we told him to draw near the fire,
An' laughed at his jest, tho' it wasn't the best,
  An' swore there's no man like McGuire.
An' when he came up with the neighbours to sup,
  His friendliness all would admire,
An' he'd have the best bed—for we'd sleep in the shed
  For fear of insulting McGuire.

But Macgilligan's Dan—who's a rale fightin' man,
  Said, "Of all this tall talkin' I tire,
I'll step in an' see whyever should he
  Be called always Fightin' McGuire.
I'll step in and say, in a casual way,
  That I think he's a thief an' a liar,
Then I'll hit him a clout, and unless I misdoubt,
  That's a way of insulting McGuire."

Then onward he strode to McGuire's abode,
  His glorious eye shootin' fire,
An' we thought as he passed we have all looked our
    last
  On the man who insulted McGuire;
Then we listened with grief while we heard him called
    thief,
An' abused as a rogue an' a liar;
Oh ! we all held our breath, for we know it was death
  To give any chat to McGuire.

Well, the row wasn't long, but 'twas hot an' 'twas
    strong,
  An' the noise it grew higher an' higher,
Then it stopt !—an' we said, " Oh, begorra, he's dead !
  He's been kilt out an' out be McGuire ! "
Then out like a thrush from a hawthorn bush
  Came something in tattered attire,
And after it fled the man we thought dead—
  The man who malthreated McGuire.

'Twas Macgilligan's son, the victory won,
  An' we crowded around to admire
The bowld-hearted boy who was first to distroy
  The Yoke of the Tyrant McGuire.
An' altho' it's not true, we all said that we knew
  From the first he was only a liar,
An' we'd all had a mind to attack—from behind—
  That cowardly scoundrel—McGuire.

CARMODY'S MARE

There's the saddlin' bell ringing! — the numbers are
    up,
Oh, man dear! I must see the race for the Cup.
Push up on that plank there! hi! gimme a hand!
Oh, man! this is better than any Grand Stand.
There's high fliers payin' a shillin'—an' two
That hasn't the half, nor the quarter the view.
Hi! Peter! McGinty! Miginty me son
Come up here an' see the big race bein' run.
—Not room for another? Oh, now you be civil
—Come up here me haro!—An' you to the divil!
Look Peter from here you can see the whole Course
—Ay, call up a policeman, call up the whole Force!
There's the bank an' the hurdles an' there's the stone
    wall.
An' there's the big water jump, best o' them all.
Who am I backin'? Well, now I declare
I've got all me money on Carmody's mare!—
—Last night it was Carmody gave me the tip
—(You'll be over the rail if ye give any ' lip ')
—He told me the ring men were at him agin
To pull the bay mare—but he's riding to win
Thirty pounds if he pulled her!—ay, that's what they
    said
An' let " Queen o' the May " come and romp in
    instead,
But he'll not take their money, he means to ride fair,
An' that's why me shirt is on Carmody's mare.

There's Carmody! gallopin' down on the bay,
There's Dimpsey, the robber! on "Queen o' the
　　May,"
There's Flynn on " The Firefly "—Burke on " Red
　　Fox,"
There's Mangan on " Merry-Legs "—see the white
　　socks,
There's Sweeny on " Swanshot "—There's Major
　　Tom Goff !
He's linin' them up, boys!—Begorra they're off!
Sit down you in front there! well take off that hat,
I'll take off yer head, if ye give any chat!
Where is he, Peter? Well up in the front?
Oh, don't say that's him at the heel o' the hunt!
Ah, sure, I know why he is keepin' her in,
Yer goin' too fast at the bank, Mr. Flynn.
Didn't I tell you, that lep is too wide
No sinsible horse, 'ill take that in his stride.
Ah! look at Carmody—Carmody knows
Hop and go lightly an' over he goes!
What's that yer sayin' there?—Heavens above!
Was there ever a race where a man didn't shove?
Fall off an' be hanged to you, little I care,
As long as Ned Carmody sticks to his mare.
Where is he, Peter?—the Hurdles! well done!
Now, see him off like the shot from a gun!
WILL you sit down, there, I must see the race,
Ye want the contints o' me fist in yer face.
Where is he, Peter! Oh! the stone wall,
Ah, Mr. Sweeny, you're out of it all.
Don't let her race at it! Keep her in check!
Or ye'll break her two legs and' yer own silly neck!
Ah! look at Carmody, sinsible chap!

Look at him goin' where Flynn made the gap.
What's that yer talkin' of? What's that you say?
The race is a mortal for " Queen o' the May!"
Oh, bedad! look at her, sailin' away,
Now, Carmody, Carmody, let out the bay,
—Slash at her, slaughter her, into her now,
'Tis the bay mare that's under you, 'tisn't a cow.
Hustle her, bustle her, drive her across,
'Tis the bay mare that's under you, 'tisn't an ass,
Now, for the Water Jump, grip wid yer thighs,
Rise the mare over it—over she flies!
Look at the two o' them into the straight,
Carmody gains on him! isn't he great?
Now, for a touch o' the spur in her flank,
—D'ye think ye've the lease o' this dirty old plank?
WILL ye go home, and take care o' yer twins?
A thousand pounds level, that Carmody wins!
Didn't I tell ye, ye ignorant calf,
Carmody wins by a lingth an' a half,
Didn't I tell it ye, Peter me son,
Carmody wins, an' I got five to one!—
An' now me good people, I'm just goin' down.
Down to the Bookie to get—me Half-crown.

SHLATHERY'S MOUNTED FUT.

You've heard o' Julius Cæsar, an' the great Napoleon,
    too,
An' how the Cork Militia beat the Turks at Waterloo ;
But there's a page of glory that, as yet, remains uncut,
An' that's the Martial story o' the Shlathery's Mounted
    Fut.

This gallant corps was organised by Shlathery's eldest
    son.

A noble-minded poacher, wid a double-breasted gun;

An' many a head was broken, aye, an' many an eye
    was shut,

Whin practisin' manœuvres in the Shlathery's Mounted
    Fut.

CHORUS.

An' down from the mountains came the squadrons an'
    platoons,

Four-an'-twinty fightin' min, an' a couple o' sthout
    gossoons,

An' whin we marched behind the dhrum to patriotic
    tunes,

We felt that fame would gild the name o' Shlathery's
    Light Dhragoons.

Well, first we reconnoithered round o' O'Sullivan's
    Shebeen—

It used to be " The Shop House," but we call it,
    " The Canteen:"

But there we saw a notice which the bravest heart un-
    nerved—

" All liquor must be settled for before the dhrink is
    served."

So on we marched, but soon again each warrior's
    heart grew pale,

For risin' high in front o' us we saw the County Jail;

An' whin the army faced about, 'twas just in time to
    find

A couple o' policemin had surrounded us behind.

CHORUS.

Still, from the mountains came the squadrons and
    platoons,
Four-an'-twinty fightin' min, an' a couple o' sthout
    gossoons;
Says Shlathery, " We must circumvent these bludge-
    onin' bosthoons,
Or else it sames they'll take the names o' Shlathery's
    Light Dhragoons.

"We'll cross the ditch," our leader cried, " an' take
    the foe in flank,"
But yells of consthernation here arose from every
    rank,
For posted high upon a tree we very plainly saw,
" Threspassers prosecuted, in accordance wid' the
    law."
" We're foiled!" exclaimed bowld Shlathery, " here
    ends our grand campaign,
'Tis merely throwin' life away to face that mearin'
    dhrain,
I'm not as bold as lions, but I'm braver nor a hin,
An' he that fights and runs away will live to fight
    agin."

CHORUS.

An' back to the mountains went the squadrons and
    platoons,
Four-an'-twinty fightin' min an' a couple o' sthout
    gossoons;
The band was playing cautiously their patriotic tunes;
To sing the fame, if rather lame o' Shlathery's Light
    Dhragoons.

THE CRUISE OF THE PIRATE 'BUS.

Sez Bill to me, " I'm beat," sez he, " I haven't a
    coin to clink,
I can't make both ends meet," sez he—" I can't
    make one end drink!"
Sez I to Bill, " There's a trump card still that hasn't
    been played by us.
We're both mechanics of nerve and skill, let's capture
    a motor 'bus."
We stole her that night; she was green and white, so
    we painted her red and blue,
And you couldn't tell where she had come from, I'll
    swear, or where she was going to.
For we painted names on her hull—"St. James," and
    " Richmond," and " Regent's Park,"
" Victoria," too, and " Waterloo," and " Kew," by
    way of a lark!

'Twas merry, 'twas merry in Oxford Street, and we
    made the taxis stare
As we bowled along to Bill's old sea song, " Hi!
    tuppence to everywhere!"
And we piled them in, then Bill would grin at their
    looks of hate and rage,
When I turned the 'bus round and the passengers
    found we had come to the end of our stage!
We were doing first rate when we shipped a freight
    of gardeners bound for Kew,
And my messmate said, " There's breakers ahead,"
    when we headed for Waterloo.

To save any fuss I beached the 'bus on an island in
the Strand,
Oh! their cries of despair as we left them there,
marooned within sight o' land!

With a fiendish shout I warped her out, what were
their woes to us?
Then we shipped a fresh crew and the red flag flew
once more from the Pirate 'Bus!
By night we'd rest in a mews out west, and there
securely hid,
Our coppers we'd count till the total amount was
close on a hundred quid!
Then a big fog come, and we drove her home to
where we had found her fust,
And I went to propose to " The Kilburn Rose," while
Bill he went on a bust.
A crime?—No doubt, if we'd been found out, we
might ha' been jugged for life.
But I told this tale by the moonlight pale—and that's
how I won my wife!

SWEET MARIE.

I've a little racin' mare called Sweet Marie,
And the temper of a bear has Sweet Marie.
But I've backed the mare to win, and on her I've all
my tin,
So we'll take a trial spin, Sweet Marie.

Hould your hoult, Sweet Marie,
If you bolt, Sweet Marie,
Sure, you'll never win the Farmers' Cup for me;
And if YOU don't pull it through, faith, I'm done,
    and so are you,
For I'll trade you off for glue, Sweet Marie.

Now, the colours that I chose for Sweet Marie
Were lavender and rose for Sweet Marie,
Och, but now, no thanks to you, sure I'm quite
    another hue,
For I'm only black and blue, Sweet Marie,
    Hould your hoult, Sweet Marie,
    If you bolt, Sweet Marie
    Sure you'll never win the Farmers' Cup for me,
    Every daisy in the dell ought to know me mighty
    well,
    For on every one I fell, Sweet Marie.

Now we're started for the Cup, my Sweet Marie
Weight for age and owners up, my Sweet Marie
Owners up just now I own, but the way you're waltz-
    ing roun'
Sure, 'twill soon be owners down, Sweet Marie.
    Hould your hoult, Sweet Marie:
    Pass the colt, Sweet Marie.
    Och, you've gone and lost the Farmers' Cup for
    me.
    You're a stayer too, I find: but you're not the
    proper kind
    For you stay too far behind, Sweet Marie.

FATHER O'CALLAGHAN.

Father Cornelius O'Callaghan,
  To most of us Father Con—
To all of us quite the kindliest man,
  That ever the sun shone on.
I mind me when I was a bit of a lad,
  He stood with me out in the cold
While I told him a curious dream I'd had,
  Of findin' a crock of gold.

O Father O'Callaghan!
  When will the dream come true?
O Father O'Callaghan,
  If anyone knows 'tis you!
And Father O'Callaghan sthrok'd me pate,
  Sez he, " The story is old—
Every one that can work and wait
  Will find his crock of gold."

Rosie Mulvany was bright as a bird,
  I lov'd her, she didn't object,
But somehow I never could bring out the word,
  That Rose had a right to expect.
I'd dream of her nightly, I'd dream she said
    " Yes,"
  Be daylight me courage was gone,
I was wore to a shadow, so in my distress,
  I went and I saw Father Con.

O Father O'Callaghan,
  Will the dream come true?
O Father O'Callaghan,
  What is a boy to do?
And Father O'Callaghan said, " See here,
  You must call in your Sunday clothes.
Say to her this, ' Will you marry me dear?'
  You can leave the rest to Rose."

We talk'd one night of the glorious days,
  When Ireland led the van,
With scholars as thick as the stars in the sky
  And work for every man.
" 'Twill come again," said Father Con,
  And his fertile fancy paints
The glorious day when the sun shines on
  A new Isle of the Saints.

O Father O'Callaghan,
  When will the dream come true?
O Father O'Callaghan,
  If anyone knows, 'tis you.
And Father O'Callaghan raised his head,
  And smil'd his humorsome smile,
" When ev'ry man learns to rule himself
  'Twill then be a saintly isle."

Father O'Callaghan's dead and gone,
  This many and many a day—
But we haven't forgot you Father Con,
  And it keeps us from goin' astray.
And so at the last great earthquake shock,
  When the trumpet's soundin' clear,
He'll guide to their God the faithful flock,
  That knew him and lov'd him here.

O Father O'Callaghan,
  When will the dream come true?
O Father O'Callaghan,
  If anyone knows 'tis you!
And Father O'Callaghan says no word,
  For he's sleepin' softly yet,
And when the Archangel's voice is heard,
  We know that he won't forget.

(By kind permission of the Publishers, Ascherberg, Hopwood & Crew, Ltd., Mortimer Street, London.)

MICK'S HOTEL.

Has anybody ever been to Mick's Hotel,
Mick's Hotel by the salt say water?
None o'yez ha' been there—just as well! Just as
    well for ye!—Oh!
If ye were an ostheridge ye might contrive
To get away from the place alive;
They charge you a dollar for a meal you couldn't
    swaller,
  And it's down by the silver sea.
Oh yes, I've been there,
Yes, I was green there,
Hoping that the waiter might perhaps attend to me
" What 's in that tureen there?"
" Soup, sir," it's been there
Never again for me.

I went up to the bedroom, but I couldn't find the soap.
" Soap! is it soap by the salt say water?"
I went to ring the bell, but I couldn't find the rope,
And the waiter says to me,
" What the divil do ye want with a bedroom bell,
Haven't you a voice, and can't you yell!"
I made the waiter holler! But it cost me a dollar
    Down by the silver sea.
Oh yes, I've been there,
Wits sure are keen there,
But I was in no humour for the lad's jocositv:
Yes, I have been there
Mick's King and Queen there.
Never again for me.

" You're waiting for your breakfast, sir, and now
        what will you take?
Fish! is it fish by the salt say water?
All gone up to Dublin, sir, before you were awake."
" Kidneys and toast and tea."
Well, now, there was a kidney, but I think it was
        last week,
Oh, the tea and the toast isn't far to seek,
And marmalade to folla', that'll cost another dollar,
    Down by the silver sea.
Oh, I have been there,
Yes, I've been seen there,
Hoping against hope for that second cup of tea.
Oh yes, I've been there,
Shall I be seen there?
Never again for me.

"You're going in the morning, and you'll want to pay
    your bill."
Bill! oh, the bill by the salt say water!
If you want to see the size of it you've got to climb
    a hill,
Or spread it on the silver sea.
They work by " double entry "—then they multiply
    by three
And still there's three and sixpence that they haven't
    got from me.
" Oh, ye washed his flannel collar, put down 'Laundry
    —one dollar!'
  Though you washed it in the silver sea."
Oh yes, I've been there,
Cleaned out quite clean there.
The waiter can't explain the bill, and Mick you never
    see.
Oh yes, I've been there,
I got quite lean there,
Never again for me.

*(By kind permission of the Publishers, Pigott & Co.,
Grafton Street, Dublin.)*

"ARE YE RIGHT THERE, MICHAEL?"

A Lay of the Wild West Clare.

You may talk of Columbus's sailing
    Across the Atlantical sea
But he never tried to go railing
    From Ennis as far as Kilkee.
You run for the train in the mornin',
    The excursion train starting at eight,
You're there when the clock gives the warnin',
    And there for an hour you'll wait.

(Spoken):

    And as you're waiting in the train,
    You'll hear the guard sing this refrain:—

" Are ye right there, Michael? are ye right?
Do you think that we'll be there before the night?
    Ye've been so long in startin',
    That ye couldn't say for sartin'—
Still ye might now, Michael, so ye might!"

They find out where the engine's been hiding,
    And it drags you to sweet Corofin;
Says the guard, " Back her down on the siding,
    There's the goods from Kilrush comin' in."
Perhaps it comes in in two hours,
    Perhaps it breaks down on the way;
" If it does," says the guard, " be the powers,
    We're here for the rest of the day!"

(Spoken):

And while you sit and curse your luck,
The train backs down into a truck!

" Are ye right there, Michael, are ye right?
Have ye got the parcel there for Mrs. White?
    Ye haven't! Oh, begorra!
    Say it's comin' down to-morra—
And it might now, Michael, so it might!"

At Lahinch the sea shines like a jewel,
    With joy you are ready to shout,
When the stoker cries out, " There's no fuel,
    And the fire's taytotally out.
But hand up that bit of a log there—
    I'll soon have ye out of the fix;
There's a fine clamp of turf in the bog there;"
    And the rest go a-gatherin' sticks.

(Spoken):

And while you're breakin' bits of trees,
You hear some wise remarks like these:—

" Are ye right there, Michael? are ye right?
Do ye think that ye can get the fire to light?"
    " Oh, an hour you'll require,
    For the turf it might be drier——"
" Well, it might now, Michael, so it might!"

Kilkee! Oh, you never get near it!
    You're in luck if the train brings you back,
For the permanent way is so queer, it
    Spends most of its time off the track.

Uphill the ould engin' is climbin',
  While the passengers push with a will;
You're in luck when you reach Ennistymon,
  For all the way home is down-hill.

(Spoken):

And as you're wobbling through the dark,
You hear the guard make this remark:—

" Are ye right there, Michael? are ye right?
Do you think that ye'll be home before it's light?"
    ." 'Tis all dependin' whether
    The ould engin' howlds together——"
"And it might now, Michael, so it might!"

(*By kind permission of the Publishers, Pigott & Co., Grafton Street, Dublin.*)

THE DARLIN' GIRL FROM CLARE.

We were sittin' on the wall upon a Sunday
To watch the girls go by,
And thinkin' we'd be marrit to one one day,
When Kate Flynn caught our eye.
Oh, man! she was the makin's of a fairy,
And it made each boyo swear,
" There's not one girl in the wide, wide world
Like the girl from the County Clare!"

  Chorus:

    And ev'ry man had got the finest plan,
    You ever see now—barrin' me now,
    Ev'ry day there's one of them would say,
    That she'll agree now,—you'll see now;

All night they'd fight,
As to which o' them was right,
In the colour of her eyes and hair,
But not a word from me was ever heard,
About the darlin' girl from Clare!

Says Fagin, " 'Tis the father I'll be plazin,'
I'll tell him of the land I've tilled,
I'll tell him of the cattle I have grazin'
And the house I mean to build;
And whin he sees the ' arable ' and ' pasture '
And the fat stock feedin' there,
An' the hens an' the chickens,
Ye may go to the dickens
For the girl from the County Clare."

Chorus:

So every man had got the finest plan
Ye ever see now—barrin' me now,
Ev'ry day there's one of them would say
That she'll agree now—you'll see now.
Thinks I " wethen now
Though I haven't ere a cow,
Of brass I've got my share,
And so I know the way they ought to go
About the darlin' girl from Clare."

Sez Sharkey, "she'll be coming to the shop there
To buy some sort of thing,
I'll ax her if she has a mind to stop there,
And should I buy the ring:
An' whin she sees the curtains on the windas,

An' the old clock on the stair
Keepin' time to the minit,
No one else will be in it
With the darlin' girl from Clare!''

Chorus:

So every man had got the finest plan
Ye ever see now—barrin' me now,
Ev'ry day there's one of them would say,
That she'll agree now—you'll see now;
Thinks I '' ye may stop
Till yer dead in yer shop,
An' not a hair she'll care,
Wid all yer gold
Ye'll never hold a hold
Upon the darlin' girl from Clare.''

I never said a single word about her,
But I met the girl that day,
I told her I could never live widout her,
An' what had she to say?
She said that I might go and see her father:
I met him then and there,
An' in less than an hour
We war fightin' for the dower
Of the darlin' girl from Clare!

Chorus:

So ev'ry man had got the finest plan
Ye ever see now—barrin' me now,
Ev'ry day there's one of them would say
That she'll agree now—you'll see now;

But late last night
When the moon was bright
I axed her if she'd share
Me joy an' me sorra'—
An' begorra! on tomorro'
I'll be married to the girl from Clare!

LADIES' VERSION.

Will ye look at them? Ah mother, the whole population of London is lookin' at me. It's like that time
at Ballinafad when they had two funerals and a
merry-go-round the same day. It's like that grand
procession in Belfast when the policeman stopped
that grand lady. " Let me pass," sez she, " I'm
the wife of a Cabinet Minister." " I can't do that,
mum," sez the bobby, " No, not if you were the wife
of a Presbyterian Minister." It's from the County
Clare I come, God help me, a cold and dissolute
country just facin' the sea. Me and mother lives
contagious to Kilrush—turn to the right a mile-and-
a-half before ye come to Finigan's—at laste it was
Finigan's till the Clancys took it over—but—Ah!
sure, anybody'll show ye. I wondher if I'll find as
many sweethearts in London as I did in Ireland. I
might now. A strange gintleman raised his hat to
me as I was walkin' along the Sthrand just now. I
was about to explain to him that he'd mistaken me
for someone else, when a policeman said, " Pass
along, there, pass along!" Three bould bachelor
boys were courtin' me when I kem to Limerick for

the winther. " The Darlin' Gurl from Clare," they
called me. Wait till I tell you the song I had about
them. (Chord.) Are ye listenin', mother?

I haven't any right to be complaining
Wid three strings to my bow,
I declare to you it's lovers it is raining!
On every bush they grow;
I'm told they talk about me night and morning,
And every boy will swear,
" There's not a pearl in the wide, wide worl'
Like the girl from the County Clare!"

Chorus:

And ev'ry man has got the finest plan
Ye ever seen now—'bout me now,
Ev'ry day there's one of them would say
That she'll agree now—you will see now;
All night they'll fight as to which had got
My property to share,   [the right
But oh! boys oh!
That's not the way to go,
To win the darlin' girl from Clare.

Says Phelim, " 'Tis the father I'll be plazin',
I'll tell him of the land I've tilled,
I'll tell him of the cattle I have grazin'
And the house I mean to build;
And whin he sees the ' arable ' and ' pasture '
And the fat stock feedin' there,
An' the hens an' the chickens,
Ye may go to the dickens
For the girl from the County Clare."

Chorus:

> So every man had got the finest plan
> Ye ever see now—'bout me now,
> Ev'ry day there's one of them would say
> That she'll agree now—you'll see now;
> Thinks I " You're grand,
> Wid your house and your land,"
> But I'm not wanting there,
> For oh! boys oh!
> That's not the way to go
> About the darlin' girl from Clare."

Sez Connor, " She'll be coming to the shop there
To buy some sort of thing,
I'll ax her if she has a mind to stop there,
And should I buy the ring;
An' whin she sees the curtains on the windas,
An' the old clock on the stair
Keepin' time to the minit,
No one else will be in it
With the darlin' girl from Clare."

Chorus:

> So ev'ry man had got the finest plar
> Ye ever see now—'bout me now,
> Ev'ry day there's one of them would say
> That she'll agree now—you'll see now,
> Thinks I, " Ye may stop
> Till yer dead in yer shop
> An' not a hair I'll care,
> Wid all your gold
> Ye'll never hold a hold
> Upon the darlin' girl from Clare."

But Shamus came and put his arms about me,
Oh! he's the right boy, too,
He told me he could never live without me,
And so what could I do!
I told him he must go and see me father,
He kissed me then and there,
And in less than an hour,
He was fighting for the dower
Of the darlin' girl from Clare.

Chorus:

So ev'ry man had got the finest plan
Ye ever see now—barrin' me now,
Ev'ry day there's one of them would say
That she'll agree now—you'll see now;
But late last night
When the moon was bright.
He axed me if I'd share
His joy an' his sorra'—
An' begorra! on to-morra'
He'll be married to the girl from Clare!

(*By kind permission of the Publishers, Joseph Williams,
Ltd., Gt. Portland St., London.*)

MATHEW HANIGAN'S AUNT.

Oh, Mat Hanigan had an aunt,
  An uncle too, likewise;
But in this chant, 'tis Hanigan's aunt
  I mean to eulogize.
For when young lovers came
  And axed her to be their's,
Mat Hanigan's aunt took each gallant
  And fired him down the stairs.

Chorus.

So here's a health to Hanigan's aunt!
  I'll tell you the reason why,
She always had things dacent
  In the Hanigan family;
A platther and can for every man,
  " What more do the quality want?
" You've yer bit and yer sup what's cockin'
    yees up!"
  Sez Mathew Hanigan's aunt.

Oh, she never could raise her voice,
  She never was known to scold,
But when Hanigan's aunt sed, " No, you
    can't,"
  You did what you were told;
And if anyone answered back,
  Oh, then his hair she'd comb,
" For all I want," sez Hanigan's aunt,
  " Is peace in our happy home."

    Chorus:—So here's a health, etc.

Oh, when she went to Court,
  The A-de-congs in vain
Would fume and rant, for Hanigan's Aunt
  Said, " Boy let go me thrain!"
And when the Lard Liftinant
  A kiss on her brow would imprint,
" Oh no, you can't," said Hanigan's Aunt
" Widout me pa's consint."

        Chorus:—So here's a health, etc.

Oh, 'tis often we'd praise her up,
  We'd laud her to the sky,
We'd all discant on Hanigan's Aunt,
  And hope she never would die.
But still, I'd like to add—
  If Hanigan isn't about—
That whin we plant Mat Hanigan's Aunt,
  We won't be too put out.

        Chorus:—So here's a health, etc.

(By kind permission of the Publishers, Pigott & Co., Grafton Street, Dublin.)

SHORT PLAYS AND DIALOGUES

THE LETTER FROM THE FRONT.

Scene: Interior of an Irish cottage.

CHARACTERS :

EILEEN O'CONNOR: *An Irish colleen, aged* 18.

MATTHEW KAVANAGH: *An elderly Irish schoolmaster.*

PROPS : *A small deal table, two chairs, writing materials, a letter, and a copy-book.*

(*Matthew discovered seated at table L. as curtain rises.*)

Mat : Oh, wirra, wirra ! why didn't them Germans declare war forty years ago, an' give me a chance. Here I am with nothing to do but write copy-heads for little gossoons that would be better employed chasing butterflies. (*Writes.*)

'' The ox saw the fox had no socks, this shocks the ox.''

Ah, let me bring these old copy heads up-to-date :

'' The Hun saw my son with a gun—he run !''

157

" The shell fell in the well and played——"
(*Knock.*)

Come in !

(*Door opens R., and Eileen puts her head in.*)

Eileen: Yer busy, Mister Kavanagh.

Mat: Maybe I am, and maybe it can wait. What's troublin' you, Eileen Oge ?

(*Eileen comes up to the table.*)

Eileen: 'Tis a letter I've got from Andra.

Mat: Oh ! the boy that went to join the colours; has he got into a scrape ?

Eileen: Oh, no ! he's doin' grand, but I want you to help me persuade him not to run his head into all them dangers.

Mat: How long is he inlisted ?

Eileen: Four weeks come Frida'.

Mat: Och ! he's in no danger.

Eileen: (*taking letter from under shawl.*) Oh ! isn't he ! Wait till I read ye the letter he's sent me. (*Jumps on table facing audience, and swings legs.*)

Mat: I don't see how he can be in any danger.

Eileen: (*reading*) " Me own heart's darlin'," (*bends down towards Matthew*) That's me. (*Matthew nods, and lights pipe.*) " Here I am in the thick of it ! " (*Matthew starts.*) On Monday I was sent to re-inforce Rooshans—"

Mat: (*Starting up to look over letter.*) Sent to what ?

Eileen: " Re-inforce the Rooshans ! You would hardly know yer Andra with the light o' battle in me eye."

Mat: " In me eye "—I think it is.

Eileen: " Waving me sword."

Mat: Me sword ! Has he a commission ?

Eileen: A commission ! Not on this job. He got 15 per cent. when he was selling pigs.

Mat: Oh, I mean—is he an officer ?

Eileen: He said he would be soon—that was four weeks ago. (*Matthew grunts.*) " I had a shot at Hindenburg—"

Mat: Hinden—— !

Eileen: " But missed him—he was running so fast, an' the light bad."

Mat: The light bad !

Eileen: " Back next morning to help the Belgums."

Mat: Next morning—quick travelling.

Eileen: " Not much of a scrap, as the Huns don't like the look of me—I haven't shaved for a week." (*To Matthew.*) He was a barefaced boy when he left.

Mat: He's a barefaced—never mind.

Eileen: " A thousand kisses to you, my heart's delight. (That's me.) There's General Joffer ringing me up on the gramaphone."

Mat: Well ! of all——

Eileen: (*Jumping off table, and coming round to back.*) An' now, Mister Kavanagh, I want you to write a reel interestin' letter to Andra.

Mat: Is it me to write a love letter?

Eileen: Oh! I'll put in the love. Hurry up now. I want to begin talkin' to him.

Mat: (*Writing.*) "Dear Andra—Butter has gone up sixpence—which is a good thing for those who have it to sell. Bakers' bread is up, too, but, thank God, we can make our own——"

Eileen: (*Who was getting more and more impatient*). Ah, I wouldn't begin that way.

Mat: Ye wouldn't?

Eileen: No, sthroke that out.

Mat: Stroke it out? (*Does so.*)

Eileen: (*Leaning arms on table and looking out at audience.*) Begin like this—" Me own darlin' little thief o' the world (sleeveen)."

Mat: Why d'you call him a robber?

Eileen: Didn't he steal me heart away?

Mat: Ay, but he left you his in its place.

Eileen: (*Hands on breast.*) An' I have it safe!

Mat: Lucky lad!

Eileen: (*Starting up.*) Lucky! an' the shells blowin' his head off every minit. " Me darlin'."

Mat: (*Writing.*) Me darlin'.

Eileen: (*Trying to think of news.*) "There's not much news to tell you——"

Mat: (*Writing.*) Tell you.

Eileen: "But I just happened to meet ould Flogthe-boys " (*starts back apologetically* ; *Matthew drops pen, and scratches his head.*) Oh, I beg yer pardon, Mister Kavanagh.

Mat : An, what harm—I never lifted the stick to you, Eileen.

Eileen: You did not, indeed. "I just happened to meet our dear ould schoolmaster—

Mat: That's better '

Eileen: "An' he tould me, me darlin'," now you go on.

Mat: (*Writing.*) "An' he tould me, me darlin'— Hogs is fetchin' a fine price——"

Eileen: " But I would rather have you, dear, than a thousand hogs."

Mat : (*Aside*) Great fall in the price of hogs (*looks off.*) Hurry up, now ! There's the postman comin' down to lift the letters.

Eileen: "Oh, my, my—a thousand kisses to you, my heart's delight."

Mat: Delight.

Eileen: "An' me pillow prayer every night is——"

Mat: Night is——

Eileen: " That God may send you safe home to yer lovin' little Eileen."

Mat: Eileen.

Eileen: (*Sigh of relief.*) D'ye think he'll like that ?

Mat: He will so. An' now (*putting letter in envelope*) all we want is the address.

Eileen: (Coming round from back of table, and taking out her lover's letter.) Oh ! the address !

Mat: (Writing.) Andra Flynn—

Eileen: Aldershott.

Mat: (Falling back) Aldershott ! ! !

Eileen: Yes, 'tis a town he tuk from the Germans the first week he joined.

Mat: A town he tuk from the Germans ! 'Tis in the heart of England—'tis a thrainin' school for soldiers.

Eileen: (Flabbergasted.) A thrainin' school for soldiers ! Then he's not fightin' !

Mat: He was always a bit of a rogue.

Eileen: (Getting angry.) An' all the time I was prayin' for him he was, maybe, sittin' in school wid a dunce's cap on his head.

Mat: He's no dunce !—the boy that wrote that letter's no dunce.

Eileen: Gimme me letter !

Mat: (Covering it with his hand as she snatches at it.) What would ye do with it ?

Eileen: I'd burn it !

Mat: Hould on, now—hould on.

Eileen: (Passionately) He's been making a fool o' me—an' all the time I thought he was a haro. *(Falls into chair, and leans on table with her head on her outstretched arms, sobbing.)*

Mat: (rising and coming to her behind table) An' Mother o' God, girl *(bangs fist on table)*, he is a haro! an' I'll tell you why. Wasn't he the brightest boy that ever passed out o' the school! Wasn't he the lad that took his mother's farm out o' the hands o' the moneylenders! Wasn't he the man they were screechin' for to be foreman o' the mill! Wasn't the whole world before him—an' then when the call came, wasn't he the first to hear that call and join the colours?

Joke! Let him have his joke!—he's not fightin' yet, but he's learnin' to fight, an' where he's goin' is no joke! God help you, girl, you don't know a hero when you see one.

Eileen: (*Who has been gradually recovering during speech.*) Gimme me letter.

Mat: You'd burn it?

Eileen: Ye haven't ere a stamp on ye?

Mat: (*Giving letter.*) Ah! good girl, good girl!

Eileen: Fightin' or no fightin', he's the boy I love, and he IS a haro!

(*Curtain might come down here, or they might EXIT on following lines—*)

Mat: Bedad! there's a pair o' ye! Come on to the post office.

G L O O M .

A Russian Hair and Curtain Raiser.

By I. KAN NOKEMOFF.

Scene: A cottage interior; moonlight through window; small table and two chairs L. C., a lighted candle in candlestick on table.

LITTLE MOTHER : *An old peasant woman discovered sitting sideways to audience—her arms stretched out on table, and her head bowed upon them. Wolves heard off.*
ENTER ZOGITOFF, *her son, carrying a book and a lighted candle; he puts candle on table.* LITTLE MOTHER *blows her candle out.* ZOG *sits facing audience and reads.*

Lit. Mother: How your voice has improved, Zogitoff.

Zog.: I was not singing, Little Mother.

Lit. M.: Sing me that melody again, Zogitoff.

Zog.: (*Irritated.*) I was *not* singing, Little Mother, it was the cry of the wolves you heard.

Lit. M.: What are they crying for ? *They* never cared for Vodka.

Zog.: They do not resemble you, Little Mother.

Lit. M.: When the war is over will they give us the Vodka again?

Zog.: Never again, Little Mother.

Lit. M.: (*Aghast*) Will we have merry-making as in the olden time—no shrieking of women—no howling of men?

Zog: There will be silence, Little Mother.

Lit. M.: (*Throwing out her arms.*) You will ıot get drunk and beat your wife?

Zog.: I will remain sober, Little Mother.

(*Wolves howl.*)

Shall I read you " The Christmas Carol " ? It is by Charles Dickensvitch.

Lit M.: No, it would tell of revelry, laughter, and the brewing of punch—I could not bear it.

(*Wolves howl.*)

(*Enter R. Orfulkoff, an asthmatic subject, and his fiancee, Little Tileoff.*)

Orf.: (*Sadly.*) A merry Christmas to you, Zogitoff ! (coughs).

Zog.: A merry Christmas to you, Orfulkoff.

Tileoff (*Sadly.*) A merry Christmas to you, Little Mother.

Lit. M.: (*Dourly.*) There can be no " merry Christmas "—there is no vodka !

Orf.: Tileoff and I are happy since the doctor diagnosed us.

Zog.: What was the doctor's diagnosis, Orfulkoff?

Orf.: We are to die to-night (*coughs*).

Tileoff: How I love that cough!

Lit. M.: There can be no funeral! There is no vodka!

Orf.: Tileoff and I will wander away into the forest—the snow will be our winding sheet.

(*Wolves howl.*)

Zog.: But the wolves will eat you.

Orf.: Poor things! they are starving.

Tileoff: Do you grudge them their food?

Zog.: He thinks of others, Little Mother; even of the wolves.

Orf.: *They* will have a merry Christmas.

Tileoff: And a happy New Year.

Zog.: (*Rising and stretching his hands towards Tileoff.*) Tileoff—little Tileoff, you loved me once.

Tileoff: Yes, when you said you had an incurable disorder.

Zog.: A wrong diagnosis. They thought it was appendicitis—it was Hay Fever.

Tileoff: (*Who has come forward, and taken his hands.*) You deceived me.

Zog.: May I die with you?

Tileoff: It is for Orfulkoff to say. (*Turns away.*)

Zog.: May I die with you?

Orf.: Yes, the wolves would prefer it.

Tileoff: If the wolves don't mind waiting.

(*Wolves howl.*)

(*They sit on floor.*)

(*During song wolves might do a bouche fermée obligato.*)

Air—" The Boatmen of the Volga."

When the Doc. said,
We'd be soon dead,
Our friends were awfully sad ;
We were quite glad,
So we bid adieu,
To all but these two,
Now we're going, they are going, too.

(*All rise and walk round stage.*)

To the forest we will slowly go,
We'll be covered by the falling snow.
So they won't know,
If we're living or dead ;
And thro' their dreaming
We'll be shapes of dread
It's a rum go,
It is some snow.   (*Wolves howl.*)

(*Exeunt.*)

Curtain.

THE CHILDREN'S PARTY,

OR

THE STORY OF THE LION THAT WOULDN'T EAT PARSLEY.

(Peter Binks enters with hair slightly dishevelled, and a worried and depressed expression.)

I have just come back from a children's party. I am one of the survivors. There are not many of us.

When I got to the house the servant asked me to leave my clothes in the hall. Of course I did not do so, but I am sorry now that I didn't—they were my best clothes; now they're not clothes at all—just garments for the poor . . . . I went into the room, and they gave me a cup of tea—the small child crawling between my legs got the cup of tea, the one climbing up the back of my chair got the saucer.

Then we fed them for a solid hour; after that one would think that they would have liked to lie down for a bit, but they didn't; we played round games then.

Have you ever played a game called " Burning House "? The children were a fire brigade—*I* was the burning house. I find you needn't confine yourself to throwing water at a burning house ; you can throw cushions or books or fireirons.

Then we played " Mad Buffalo " ; the children were a pack of wolves—*I* was the mad buffalo. I'm glad I wasn't born a mad buffalo, it has a weary life. Most of its time is spent under the sofa avoiding wolves . . . . Then they said, " let's play ' Dragging the Pond' !" I came out from under the sofa and said, " No, children, we won't play ' Dragging the Pond ' '' (I knew who was going to be the pond), " But I'll tell you a story instead." I thought it would keep them quiet, and I didn't know how hard it is to tell stories to small children. You see, they interrupt you so, and ask so many questions, and want all the particulars.

(*With one foot on a chair, and as if surrounded by children on the floor.*)

Now, children, you sit down there, and I'll tell you the story. Just there—oh ! anywhere. Yes, UNDER the carpet if you like—stop biting my leg !

(*Sits on back of chair with feet on the seat.*)

No, it's not more comfortable up here, but's it's safer. Yes, away from the wolves. . . . . Well, there was once an old woman—no the

old woman wouldn't eat you—yes, a lion would
EAT you—oh ! yes, there's a lion in the story—
yes, a tiger 's worse—yes, a lion 's worse than a
tiger ; well, HE said it first dear, he said it FIRST.

Well, the old woman lived in a wood. No, there
were no lions in the wood. Oh ! the next wood was
full of lions—yes, and tigers too, bulging out of the
tops of the trees—they couldn't come down on
account of the lions.

Well, the old woman had a son called Jack, and
—NO ! Jack wouldn't eat you—I wish he would—
yes, we're coming to the lion now—

The old woman sent Jack down to water the
garden. . . . What ? . . . . Oh ! the usual sort of
garden. Roses and spinach and polyanthuses, and
—yes, there was lots of parsley in the garden.

No, a lion wouldn't eat parsley ; he'd eat Jack
without it—glad to get him.

So Jack went down to the well—

NO ! THERE WERE NO TIGERS IN THE
SPINACH ! Yes, but a blackbird isn't a tiger !
Besides spinach is green and a tiger is yellow ; the
gardener would have noticed a tiger if there'd been
one—Yes, he was a very careful man—a Scotch—
yes, he had two rakes, one for slugs, and one for
tigers.

So Jack went down to the well—yes, we're
coming to the lion—yes, the lion's in the well !
When Jack came down, there was a GREAT BIG

LION sitting in the well—yes, on the water . . . .
I SAID he was on the water, and he WAS on
the water ! . . . . I don't care ! Lions DON'T
sink ! . . . . They have some way—yes, they
waggle their tails underneath. They tread water
with their tails.

And Jack ran to his mother, and said : "There's
a great big lion sitting in the well !" And she said :
" You silly boy, that's not a lion, it's your Uncle
Thomas." So Jack went back to the well, but
he found that it wasn't Uncle Thomas, but it WAS
a great big lion ; and it jumped out of the well, and
gobbled him up.

The Moral ? . . . . Oh ! the moral is that if you
believe all your mother tells you, you'll be eaten by
a great big lion.

EXAMINATION FOR THE POST OF EDITOR OF *IRISH CYCLIST*.

This exam. was held at 49 Middle Abbey Street, during the temporary absence of the Editor. The candidates were " Graphis," " Philander," "Will Wagtale," and the Office Dog, and the result (a free fight) is published in to-day's police reports.

We subjoin a list of questions.

PAPER A.—ANCIENT HISTORY.

1.—Give reasons for the supposition that Tyre and Sidon should be spelt Tyre and Seddon.

2.—In what year B.C. did R. J. commence cycling?

3.—Have Nero and Diogenes ever been superseded as cranks?

4.—The Pyramids of Egypt held records ; state what times they record?

B.—MECHANICS.

5.—If two bounders collide with a body going in the opposite direction, reduce the language used to its lowest terms.

6.—What form of energy is known as " The Force " ?

C.—Translation.

7.—The Abbé Grostête has purchased a bicycle ; he is abber'er (ploos hooroo) than ever.

He has conducted it to the summit of a mountain (montang).
The spokes glitter in the sun.
Nature smiles, his friends grin.
The Abbé mounts, the bike wobbles, his friends are convulsed.
The bicycle gets his head, the Abbé loses his.
His funeral is to-morrow (demang).

THE FIRST LORD LIEUTENANT.

An Historical Sketch.

As related by Andrew Geraghty (Philomath).

" Essex," said Queen Elizabeth, as the two of them sat at breakwhist in the back parlour of Buckingham Palace; " Essex, me haro, I've got a job that I think would suit you. Do you know where Ireland is ?"

" I'm no great fist at jografy," says his Lordship, " but I know the place you mane. Population, three million ; exports, emigrants."

" Well," says the Queen, " I've been reading the Dublin *Evening Mail,* and the *Telegraft,* for some time back, and sorra one o' me can get at the troot o' how things is goin', for the leadin' articles is as contradictory as if they wor husband and wife."

" That's the way wid papers all the world over," says Essex. " Columbus told me it was the same in Amirikay when he was there, abusin' and contra-dictin' each other at every turn—it's the way they make their livin'. Thrubble you for an egg spoon."

" It's addled they have me betune them," says the Queen. " Not a know I know what's going on. So now what I want you to do is to run over to Ireland, like a good fella, and bring me word how matters stand."

" Is it me?" says Essex, leppin' up off his chair. " It's not in airnest ye are, ould lady. Sure it's the hoight of the London season. Everyone's in town, and Shake's new fairy piece, ' The Mid-summer's Night Mare,' billed for next week."

" You'll go when yer told," says the Queen, fixin' him with her eye, " if you know which side yer bread's buttered on. See here, now," says she, seein' him chokin' wid vexation and a slice of corned beef, " you ought to be as pleased as Punch about it, for you'll be at the top of the walk over there as vice-regent representin' me."

" I ought to have a title or two," says Essex, pluckin' up a bit. " His Gloriosity of Great Pan-janthrum, or the like o' that."

" How would ' His Excellency the Lord Lieutenant of Ireland strike you?" says Elizabeth.

" First class," cries Essex. " Couldn't be betther ; it doesn't mean much, but it's allitherative, and will look well below the number on me hall door."

Well, boys, it didn't take him long to pack his clothes and start away for the Island o' Saints. It took him a good while to get there though, through not knowing the road ; but by means of a pocket compass, and a tip to the steward, he was landed at last contagious to Dalkey Island.

Going up to an ould man who was sitting on a rock he took off his hat, and says he :

" That's grand weather we're havin' ? "

" Good enough for the times that's in it, " says the ould man, cockin' one eye at him.

" Any divarshan goin' on ? " says Essex.

"You're a stranger in these parts, I'm thinkin'," says the ould man, " or you'd know this was a ' band night ' in Dalkey."

" I wasn't aware of it, " says Essex. " The fact is, " says he, " I only landed from England just this minute. "

" Aye, " says the old man, bitterly, " it's little they know about us over there. I'll howld you, " says he, with a slight thrimble in his voice, " that the Queen herself doesn't know there's to be fire-works in the Sorrento Gardins this night. "

Well, whin Essex heard that, he disremembered entirely that he was sent over to Ireland to put down rows and ructions, and haway wid him to see the fun and flirt with all the pretty girls he could find.

And he found plenty of them—thick as bees they were, and each one as beautiful as the day and the morra.

He wrote two letters home next day—one to Queen Elizabeth and the other to Lord Montaigle, a play-boy like himself.

I'll read you the one to the Queen first.

DAME STREET,
April 16, 1599.

FAIR ENCHANTRESS,

I wish I was back in London, baskin' in your sweet smiles and listenin' to your melodious voice once more. I got the consignment of men and the post office order all right. I was out all morning looking for the inimy, but sorra a taste of Hugh O'Neill or his men can I find. A policeman at the corner of Nassau Street told me they were hiding in Wicklow. So I am making up a party to explore the Dargle on Easther Monda. The girls here are as ugly as sin, and every minite of the day I do be wishing it was your good-looking self I was gazin' at instead of these ignorant scare-crows.

Hoppin' soon to be back in ould England, I remain, your loving subjec,

ESSEX.

P.S.—I hear Hugh O'Neill was seen on the top of the Donnybrook tram yesterday mornin'. If I have any luck the head'll be off him before you get this.—E.

The other letter read this way.

DEAR MONTY,

This is a great place all out. Come over here if you want fun. Divil such play-boys ever I seen, and the girls—oh, don't be talkin'—'pon me secret honour you'll see more loveliness at a tay and

supper ball in Ra'mines than there is in the whole
of England. Tell Ned Spenser to send me a love-
song to sing to a young girl who seems taken wid
my appearance. Her name's Mary, and she lives
in Dunlary, so he oughtent to find it hard.

I hear Hugh O'Neill's a terror, and hits a
powerful welt, especially when you're not lookin'.
If he tries any of his games on wid me, I'll give
him in charge.   No brawling for yours truly,

ESSEX.

Well, me bould Essex stopped for odds of six
months in Dublin, purtending to be very busy sub-
jugatin' the country, but all the time only losin'
his time and money without doin' a hand's turn,
and doin' his best to avoid a ruction with " Fightin'
Hugh."

If a messenger came in to tell him that O'Neill
was campin' out on the North Bull, Essex would
up stick and away for Sandycove, where, after
draggin' the Forty-foot Hole, he'd write off to
Elizabeth, sayin' "that owing to their suparior
knowledge of the country, the dastard foe had once
more eluded him."

The Queen got mighty tired of these letters,
especially as they always ended with a request to
send stamps by return, and told Essex to finish up
his business, and not to be makin' a fool of himself.

" Oh, that's the talk, is it ?" says Essex. "Very
well, me ould sauce-box " (that was the name he

had for her ever since she gev him the clip on the
ear for turnin' his back on her). " Very well, me
ould sauce-box," says he, " I'll write off to O'Neill
this very minit, and tell him to send in his lowest
terms for peace at ruling prices." Well, the treaty
was a bit of a one-sided one.

The terms proposed were : —

1. Hugh O'Neill to be King of Great Britain.

2. Lord Essex to return to London and remain
there as Viceroy of England.

3. The O'Neill family to be supported by
Government, with free passes to all theatres and
places of entertainment.

4. The London markets to buy only from Irish
dealers.

5. All taxes to be sent in stamped envelope,
directed to H. O'Neill, and marked " private."
Cheques crossed and made payable to H. O'Neill.
Terms cash.

Well, if Essex had had the sense to read through
this treaty, he'd have seen it was of too graspin' a
nature to pass with any sort of a respectable
sovereign, but he was that mad that he just stuck
the document in the pocket of his pot-metal over-
coat, and haway wid him hot foot for England.

" Is the Queen within ?" says he to the butler,
when he opened the door of the palace. His
clothes was that dirty and disorthered wid travellin'

all night, and his boots that muddy, that the butler was for not littin' him in at the first go-off. So says he very grand :

"Her Meejisty is abow stairs, and can't bee seen till she'd had her brekwish."

" Tell her the Lord Liftinant of Oirland desires an enterview," says Essex.

" Oh, beg pardon, me lord," says the butler, steppin' to one side. " I didn't know 'twas your-self was in it ; come inside, sir ; the Queen's in the dhrawin' room."

Well, Essex leps up the stairs, and into the dhrawin' room wid him, muddy boots and all ; but no sight of Elizabeth was to be seen.

" Where's your missus ?" says he to one of the maids of honour that was dustin' the chimbley-piece.

" She's not out of her bed yet," says the maid, with a toss of her head ; " but if you write your message on the slate beyant, " I'll see——" but before she had finished, Essex was up the second flight and knockin' at the Queen's bedroom door.

" Is that the hot wather ?" says the Queen.

" No ; it's me—Essex. Can you see me ?"

" Faith, I can't," says the Queen. " Howld on till I draw the bed curtains. Come in, now," says she, " and say your say, for I can't have you stoppin' long you young Lutharian."

." Bedad, yer Majesty," says Essex, droppin'

on his knees before her (the delutherer he was), " small blame to me if I am a Lutharian, for you have a face on you that would charum a bird off a bush."

" Hold your tongue, you young reprobate," says the Queen, blushing up to her curl papers wid delight, " and tell me what improvements you med in Ireland."

" Faith I taught manners to O'Neill," cries Essex.

" He had a bad masther then," says Elizabeth, looking at his dirty boots ; " couldn't you wipe yer feet before ye desthroyed me carpets, young man ?"

" Oh, now," says Essex, " is it wastin' me time shufflin' about on a mat you'd have me, when I might be gazin' on the loveliest faymale the world ever saw."

" Well," says the Queen, " I'll forgive you this time, as you've been so long away, but remimber in future, that Kidderminster isn't oilcloth. Tell me," says she, " is Westland Row station finished yet ?"

" There's a side wall or two wanted yet, I believe," says Essex.

" What about the Loop Line," says she.

" Oh, they're gettin' on with that," says he, " only some people think the girders is a disfigure-mint to the city."

" Is there any talk about the esplanade from Sandycove to Dunlary ?"

" There's talk about it, but that's all," says Essex, " 'twould be an odious fine improvement to house property, and I hope they'll see to it soon."

" Sorra much you seem to have done beyant spending me men and me money. Let's have a look at that threaty I see stickin' out of your pocket."

Well, when the Queen read the terms of Hugh O'Neill, she just gave him one look, and jumping from off the bed, put her head out of the window, and called out to the policeman on duty—" Is the Head below ? "

" I'll tell him you want him, ma'am," says the policeman.

" Do," says the Queen.

" Hullo," says she, as a slip of paper dropped out of the dispatches. " What's this ! " ' Lines to Mary.' Ho ! ho ! me gay fella, that's what you've been up to, is it ? "

Mrs. Brady's
A widow lady,
And she has a charming daughter I adore;
She's such a darlin'
She's like a starlin',
And in love with her I'm getting more and more.
Her name is Mary,
She's from Dunlary;
And her mother keeps a little candy store.

" That settles it," says the Queen. " It's the gaoler you'll serenade next."

When Essex heard that, he thrimbled so much that the button of his cuirass shook off and rowled under the dressin' table.

" Arrest that man ! " says the Queen when the Head-constable came to the door. " Arrest that thrater," says she, " and never let me set eyes on him again."

And, indeed, she never did, for soon after that he met his death from the blow of an axe he got when he was standin' on Tower Hill.

THE END.

MY FRIEND FINNEGAN.

WHEN an artist goes to sketch in the West of Ireland, there is often trouble in getting a suitable place to stay in. There are lodgings that advertise bed and board for five shillings, but you can't tell very often which is the bed and which is the board.

Generally, I put in a night at Peter Finnegan's Hotel. Peter is an important man in the locality, and a great friend of mine, and though his four-poster bed is really a tripod, and wants the least taste of the window sill to make it a permanent structure, and though by long usage the hens have established a right of way through the coffee room, these little drawbacks count for nothing ; for Peter to me is a permanent joy.

" Did you ever remark," he said to me one day, " that the three best drinks are in one syllable ? Well, it's a fact—port, clar't, and spirits."

We were looking out of the window at a new house being built, when Peter commented : —

" 'Twould be a great addition to that house, if that gable was taken away."

He certainly has a quaint way of putting things.

Finnegan runs the hotel on lines of his own. The bells generally don't work ; if you want to attract attention you have to go out and throw your hat at

them. An English visitor, having at last secured
a reply, asked for some water.

" There is no carafe in my room," he said, " no
water bottle."

" Well now," commented Finnegan ; " and I
always thought a giraffe was a bird."

The same visitor had trouble the next morning
with the boots.

" Look at my shoes," he said. " I put them
out last night, and nobody has touched them."

" That's the sort of hotel we keep," was the
answer. " Ye might put yer gold watch outside,
and nobody would touch it ! "

Finnegan is now a Justice of the Peace, and has
some good stories of the courts. When I was last
there, he had just come home from Limerick.

" There was a judge came down there a short
while ago," he told me, " and after looking round
the court he said to his solicitor, ' Where's Peter
Dillon ?' ' Lifted his little finger too often,' said
the solicitor. ' And John Carey ?' says the judge.
' Came in for money an' gave every penny of it
to the publicans.' ' And Luke Flynn ?' says the
judge. ' Sociable old fella,' says the solicitor,
' went the same road.' ' An' do ye all die of drink
here ?' says the judge. ' Ah, no,' says the solicitor,
' about three years ago there was a Christian
Brother died o' pneumonia.' "

" An' there was another old man," added
Finnegan, " died from trying to swallow a lump o'

sugar. There was a kettle of scaldin' water on the fire at the time, and they never thought of pourin' it down his throat. I told the Doctor about it afterwards, and all he said was that the man was dead enough as it was.''

One day the local poacher, Larry the Trout, came in after dinner in obedience to a summons from Finnegan, J.P., and this was their dialogue:

'' Now, Larry, I have four priests coming to dinner here on Wednesday, and what I want from you is a brace o' phaysants and a twelve-pound salmon by Tuesday.''

'' Oh, Mr. Finnegan, where in the world would I get the like o' them at this time o' year; shure the water bailiffs and keepers would have me destroyed.''

'' Tell me, Larry, is that case of assault the police have agin ye settled yet?''

'' 'Twill be up at the Petty Sessions next Wednesday, sir.''

'' Just so, Larry, and I'll be on the bench; I hear 'tis a bad case. I'll be in two minds whether to send ye up to the assizes, or to dismiss the case for want of evidence.''

'' Oh, Mr. Peter, ye wouldn't have me in jail for the races of Ballymacad!''

'' I would not, Larry, but justice must be done; and the man who wouldn't oblige an old friend to the amount of a couple of phaysants and a twelve-pound fish—such a man, I say, might easily be guilty of manslaughter!''

'' Oh, now, sir, 'twas a common assault.''

'' Manslaughter I make it, Larry, and that will be me sacrit opinion till Tuesday night, ay, and maybe after.''

.　　.　　.　　.　　.　　.

I dined with the priests on Wednesday, and Finnegan informed me, as he passed the cucumber, that Larry the Trout was still at large through want of evidence.

One day I went down to the Petty Sessions court to see Peter dispensing justice. As we went in, he asked of a constable we passed :

'' What about that case of larceny, constable ?''

'' After a fruitless search, Mr. Finnegan, all the money was recovered, barrin' one pair of boots.''

We went into the court, and Peter disposed himself upon the bench.

''What's the case, constable ?''

'' Cross summons for assault, yer worship. Dispute about a turf-bank. John Muldoon, of Carrawallen *versus* James McHugh and Mary Anne McHugh, both of Coryglass. From information received, I proceeded at the hour of between 11 and 12 a.m. to the house of John Muldoon. I found him in bed, with a towel tied round his head. I examined him for wounds or abrasions, but could find none, excepting where his head was broken in by some blunt instrument resembling, or of the nature of, an iron pot. (*Kawk, kawk, kawk* !) Put out that hen there !—Gets in thro' the winda yer worship. I told the plumber about that broken pane two months ago. I then proceeded to Coryglass. I found James McHugh in great disorder of mind and body ; he said he had been drowned in a bog-hole, and could not talk. Yes, sir, his sister could talk—she's a great masterpiece of a woman, sir."

" Call John Muldoon. Now, John, what have you to say for yourself ?"

" It was last Wensda comadas——"

" When was that ?"

" Eight days ago last Wensda, sir. I was pershuin' a goat of Paddy Pat's down to the Carrawallen bog——"

" Paddy Pat's ?"

" Young Pat Meehan, sir. That goat has me persecuted !"

" Is this a case of trespass or assault ?"

" Assault, sir, by that outrageous combustible of a woman——"

" Never mind how she strikes you."

" I wouldn't mind, sir, if she didn't strike me wid an iron pot, and me only tellin' her what she was !"

" Where was this ?"

" I'm tellin' you, sir. Down at the Carrawallen bog. I was layin' turf."

" I thought you were chasing a goat?"

" That's what had her mad with me, sir. Ye see, Paddy Pat's her nevya. An' the goat, not knowin' the harsh sort of woman she is, went to butt one of the childer—Maureen she has her called, afther the sister that went to America—"

" Yes, yes—you were laying——" .

" Layin' turf—no sir, not layin' eggs—makin' mud turf, sir, when this bombastical ould termagent comes tearin' down the boreen, and this lopsided James McHugh, sir, begins kickin' the turf back into the bog-hole——"

" Ye lie !"   (*Voice in court.*)

" Ye did, ye robber !"

" Address the court."

" Yes, sir, I'll talk to you. I wouldn't be seen talkin' to him at all. So I gave him a shove, sir ; yes, it was with the shovel I gave him the shove— I'll tell you no lie, sir—and over he went into the bog-hole. I'd ha' pulled him out, if his sisther hadn't molested me wid her iron pot."

" Well, Mr. McHugh, is Mr. Muldoon telling the truth ?"

" He's makin' an offer at it, sir, but I'd not say he was an expert. What I sez to him was—' Ye have no right to be takin' the bread and butter, let alone the turf, out of a man's mouth,' sez I ; and if me sisther hadn't restrained him wid the iron pot, I'd ha' been drowned to a nicety."

" Well, prisoners at the bar—or whatever the divil ye call yourselves—this seems to me a case of *E pluribus unum, aut Cæsar, aut nullus, Poeta nascetur non fit,* as the law books say ; which means that this case should never have come into court at all. One party has the iron pot, and the other has the shovel. Go out now, the two of ye, and settle it peaceably between yerselves, and the survivor— if any—can appear before me next Wednesday. The court is adjourned."

Though Finnegan is a great success as a magistrate, I think he is at his best when buying a pig. Last time I was with him, I accompanied him to the Market Square on fair day and witnessed a bargaining battle between him and Mr. Clancy, of Killinavat. On these occasions, the two sides start at widely divergent prices, and work slowly towards one another.

Finnegan strolled up : " Morra, Clancy ; and what brings you to the fair ? That wan ? Oh, now, you're not trying to sell that wan ? Not this fair, anyway. Well, now, as a matter of curiosity, what have you the audacity to ask for that outrage ?

" £5 ! £5 ! Hear that, ye saints in glory ! An' is it a golden pig from the Imparial ragions of the Aist ye want me to buy, or is it that dirty little runt that you brought home from the fair of Ballinasloe ? What will I give ?—does the hay-rope go wid her ? —I'll say 15s.—for bones and bristles. The fattest pig in the fair ! An' I thought it was a greyhound !

'Twould look well in the Waterloo Cup. 'Twould not be so long catching a hare—anyhow she'll not catch me. I'll say a pound.

" £3 for the worst offer at a pig in Ireland! What's that? The best pig in Ireland? God help Ireland! £2 10s. would be highway robbery, with intent to deceive by gross misrepresentation, perjury and extortion. What's that you say? An ornymint for any man's fireside, and fit for any society? Why I can only see her sideways!

" I'll not say £2 5s. That ould transparency! I'd be disgraced forever if I was seen trying to get her home before she dies of destitution. . . . . I'll say £2. Done!—and done;—Come in, now, till we wet the bargain. Sure don't I know a good pig when I see her. I've had me eye on her this while back!"

MICHAEL O'RYAN GETS THE PENSION

An Irish Sketch

CHARACTERS:

MRS. MULHORAN; Of the shop-house and post
 office.
JULIA : Her untrained assistant.
MICHAEL O'RYAN : Ballad singer.

Scene: The parlour of the shop-house, Ballyboden.

Time: Evening.

*(Julia, discovered sitting on table darning a stock-
ing.)* *(She sings.)*

" We met, 'twas in a crowad,
    An' I thought that he would shun me,
For his looks were cold and prowad,
    And his smile it was undone me."

Mrs. M.: (Off) Julia !
Julia: What is it, ma'am ?
                    (Enter Mrs. Mulhoran R.)
Mrs. M.: Didn't I tell ye to turn on the gas
half an hour ago ?
Julia: So I did ma'am, can't you smell it ?

Mrs. M.: (*Gasping*) Mother o' Heaven, ye'll have us all disthroyed !

> (*Runs across and exits L.*)

Julia: (*Singing*)
> " For him I broke the lawas
> When we fled wid wan another,
> Oh, thou hast been the cause
> Of this anguish me mother."

> (*Re-enter Mrs. M.*)

Mrs. M.: Quit that ould croonawn, and listen to me. I seen Michael O'Ryan down the street just now. How much does he owe us ?

Julia: I think 'tis squeezin' up to three shillins'.

Mrs. M.: That's enough ! No more credit, mind. (*Michael O'Ryan heard singing off.*)
There, that's him—now, mind what I told ye. A stout man like that should be at work, and not whimperin' ballads on the sthreets.

> (*Enter Michael O'Ryan C.*)

O'Ryan: God save all here.

Julia: God save you kindly, Michael.

O'Ryan: A saft evenin', Mrs. Mulhoran.

> (*Mrs. M. turns away.*)

'Tis indeed, ma'am. (*Aside to Julia*). Maybe a bit of a song would melify the situation. (*Sings*)
> " 'Twas on a windy night
> That Mr. Barney Brallaghan,
> Thought it was only right
> To call on Mistress Callaghan;

The girl was safe in bed,
    In bed the divil doubt of it,
And these were the words he said,
    That brought her bundling out of it.''

Mrs. M.: Quit that noise !

O'Ryan: What's that you say, ma'am?

Mrs. M.: Quit that noise !

O'Ryan: An' is it talking to the dog you are, or is it to Michael O'Ryan, lineal descendant of the Kings of Ireland ?

Mrs. M.: (*Sarcastically*) Who'd ha' thought it !

O'Ryan: Oh, I mind the time whin it was ''come in an' have an air o' the fire, Michael, sing us a song, Michael,''—an' now 'tis ''Quit yer noise !''

Well, I can take a hint as well as the next man. I'll take tuppence worth o' tabacca, Julia girl, an' then I'll be steppin' home.

Julia: Have yer the tuppence about you, Michael ?

O'Ryan: Have I the tuppence about me ! (*Searches pockets*) Have I the tuppence—I declare 'tis an insult to be alive in this house—have I the tuppence ?—well, I have not, then, but I'll have it next week, plaze God.

Julia: (*Pointing to Mrs. M.*) No money—no goods.

O'Ryan: So them's the orders ! Oh, she's a hard one—I'm not blaming you, Julia. (*To Mrs. M.*) Maybe I might have a look at the paper, ma'am—or is that also beyond me manes ?

Mrs. M.: Don't be takin' it haway wid ye.

O'Ryan: No, I'll not be takin' it away wid me. Quit yer noise—Have ye the tuppence—Don't be takin' it away wid ye. Oh, it's aisy seeing I'm down in the wurruld !

Mrs. M.: There's people that work—an' there's people that's only parashoots on others.

O'Ryan: Paracides is the word ye want, ma'am.

Mrs. M.: Maybe it is, God knows you ought to know !

O'Ryan: We were great people wansht—did I ever tell ye, Julia ?

Julia: Ye did, indeed, Michael ! How the O'Ryans were kings o' Connaught——

Mrs. R.: Robbin' and murtherin' all before them.

O'Ryan: They had the possisshun to keep up. Fine open-hearted men and weemin' they wor—*they* didn't grudge an honest man a read o' the paper.

Mrs. M.: They had no paper—those times.

O'Ryan: (Exasperated) Well, you have it now.

Mrs. M.: We have the paper, but I don't see the honest man.

Julia: Let him be ma'am. He'll read us the news anyways.

O'Ryan: (Reading paper) '' The Farmer's Intelligence and Ballyboden Banner of Liberty.'' The smaller the paper the bigger the name. I seen a

paper the other day called *The Times*. I declare
to God ye could ha' gone to bed in it.

" Speech on the Drainage, by Dionysius Finerty,
Esq., J.P.

" Men of Ballyboden! Standing as I do with
one foot firmly imbedded in the whirlpool of political
agitation, an' the other buried to the hilt in the
quagmire of municipal reform, am I to see our
noble river torn up by the roots, and its ashes scattered to the four winds of Heaven! "

Julia : That's great language entirely! What
does it mean I wonther ?

Mrs. M. : Oh, if you knew that, an' had yer
supper, ye might go to yer bed.

O'Ryan : " Sessions Court—Continued from page
four. The assault case. Cross-examined by Coun-
cillor Murphy ' Were you present when the prisoner
struck you ? ' ' I was.' " Wonderful the way he
worms the truth out o' them !

Julia : Aye, indeed.
O'Ryan : " The Battle of Waterloo." Is this this
week's paper, Julia?

Julia : It is, then.

O'Ryan : " The Battle of Waterloo is now a
thing of the past "—I was thinkin' so—" but
Napoleon might have succeeded if he had fed his
troops on Parker's Pink Pills for Pale Patriots—"
Oh, Blakins! 'tis only an advertisement. " Our
Serial Story—' Cursed wid a Coronet.' " Have ye
been readin' this, girl ?

Julia : I have then.

O'Ryan : I think the jook will let Lord Arthur marry Norah afther all.

Mrs. M. : Them jooks never knows their own minds from wan chapther to another.

O'Ryan : " ' S'death, ' cried the old nobleman, 'this infatuation for my son must cease! Here girl is a bottle of poison, drink it, and make me your friend for life.' "

Mrs. M. : Well, of all—!

O'Ryan : " With a cry of despair the be-autiful ballet girl hit him a crack on the jaw—(loud laughter)."

Julia : The saints preserve us !

O'Ryan : Hould on, I'm in the police news. " The beautiful girl sprang into her lover's arms, who covered her with kisses—to be continued.
" Robbery at Ballyboden House. After a fruitless search all the money was recovered, except one pair of boots.
" King George in Ireland. Great loyal demonstration. Enthusiastic reception. The Lord Mayor welcomes His Majesty, " God help him. An' who's King George, I'd like to know !

Julia : King of England, you know he got the place when his father died.

O'Ryan : Oh, I know he's King of England, but how did he become King of Ireland? What right has he to the trone of Ireland as long as me and me sister's alive?

Mrs. M.: Oh, blatherumskite!

O'Ryan: Blatherumskite yerself! If I had him here I'd talk to him. I've a mind to write to him about it.

Julia: Well, now that reminds me! there's a letter here for yerself since yesterday. 'Tis on His Majesty's Service. (*Hands letter to Michael.*)

O'Ryan: (*Handing letter*) Well, I wonther what the Govermint has agin me?

Mrs. M.: I've heard of people bein' arrested for obtainin' goods under false pretences.

O'Ryan: Do yer think is it that, Julia?

Julia: Sergeant Kilrane would ha' made that a personal affair, Michael.

O'Ryan: I doubt he would.

Mrs. M.: Maybe 'tis an abdication from King George handin' over the trone of Ireland to Michael O'Ryan, of Killinavat.

O'Ryan: Well, if it is, Julia, you'll be the first one I'll ask to be me Royal Consort.

Julia: Is that a respectable situation for a girl?

O'Ryan: 'Tis the same as a wife only they call them consorts in them latitudes. Come now, is it a bargain?

Julia: 'Tis an ould husband I'd have.

O'Ryan: Fifty-five to the minute—no more.

Julia: Fifty-five is a great age, Michael.

O'Ryan: For a woman maybe—but not for a man. "A man's a man for a' that," as the good buke says.

Julia: Well, let's see what's in the letter first.

O'Ryan: Maybe yer right. It might be only wan o' them birthday honours. Howly pewther what's this ? An order for 5s. ! Oh, be this an' be that, this must be the old age pension that Finerty wrote about. Well, well, I never thought I'd get it, I thought they'd want to know what me rale age was, or some such hocus pocus. I wonder what age he put me down—76 ! Oh, tell a good one while yer at it ! (*Rising.*)

I'll take a shillin's worth o' that tabacca Julia, girl, an' I think there's a small account against me of a few shillins'. Take it out o' the change. No, I don't want any of it. I think I'll start a deposit account here.

Julia: King George might ha' done the dacent thing—

O'Ryan: Don't say a word agin' King George, he's a right fella'. A wise and salubrious monarch, and knows well who desarves a pinshin. (*Pompously.*)

Well, having regulated me affairs, I will now make a vacation of the premises where I arrived without enthusiasm, and depart without any manifestations of uncontrollable grief or regret.

Mrs. M.: What a hurry yer in, Michael !

Julia: Take an air o' the fire !

Mrs. M.: Stop an' have a cup of tay !

Julia: Sing us a song, Michael !

O'Ryan: What a hurry yer in, Michael ! Have an air o' the fire, Michael ! Have a cup o' tay, Michael !

Sing us a song, Michael! (*Breaks down.*) 'Tis the ould times come back agin! Did I ever say a crass word to ye?

Mrs. M.: Never, Michael—not one!

O'Ryan: I doubt yer a liar, but lave it so. Julia, did ye say sing us a song?

Julia: I did, Michael. Give us a blast of " Come Back Paddy Reilly."

O'Ryan: Ah, that wants the chorist girl. Wait a while—is there some o' the neighbours out there, Julia?

Julia: (*Shading her eyes*) There are then.

O'Ryan: (*Addressing orchestra*) Men of Ballyboden, you have doubtless heard that I am in receipt of a government pension; under these melifluous circumstances I will ask you to join me in a—stop—in a chorus. (*Looks up at the gallery.*)

Friends at a distance will please accept this notice.

Song—O'Ryan.

" Come back, Paddy Reilly."

(*During song Mrs. M. and Julia get tea ready quietly. At the end of the song Julia dusts a chair and places it for O'Ryan.*)

Mrs. M.: (*As O'Ryan sits down to his tea*) Long life to you, Michael.

Julia: Success to you, Michael.

O'Ryan: 'Tis the old times come agin!

Curtain.

LARKSMEAD SCHOOL BREAKS UP

Do you remember your first school, as a small boy ? I will give you an impression of prize-giving day at mine. At the end of my first term my head was in a complete muddle, and if I had been asked suddenly whether it was Columbus or Catherine of Aragon who won the battle of Hastings, I wouldn't have answered straight off—I'd have had to think.

I wasn't quite at the bottom of the class; there was young Dodder, who knew absolutely nothing—that just kept me in my place. There were only twelve of us, all told, and according to ancient custom every boy had to get a prize. It was difficult sometimes to say why a boy should get a prize. I had done equally badly in all subjects, so they gave me the prize for general improvement. The good conduct prize was reserved for the dullest.

The prizes were laid out on a table covered with a red cloth—to hide the ink spots—and were presented to us by a local lady magnate, with an almost inaudible voice. The Head (and only) Master came pompously forward, in his cap and gown, and led off with a few remarks :

Lady Jumbletop and boys of the Larksmead School ! Now that you are all assembled here, and I see you for the last time before the holidays (that applause, Dodder, is somewhat ill-timed), I am pleased to tell you that the progress made this term is, on the whole, satisfactory.

In the history class. There were one or two answers in your paper, Daftie, which I don't quite follow.

You say that every Gaul was divided into three parts, and you assert that Cæsar was a very strong man, because he threw a bridge across the Rhine. Also, you make a statement that Mary Queen of Scots would have succeeded to the English throne if her mother had been a man. The History Prize has been awarded to Master Archibald Owlett, the Head of the School. (There is loud applause when he comes up for his prize, because he can lick any boy in the room.)

Lady Jumbletop murmurs:

" ' Creasy's Decisive Beetles.' "

" Battles, Lady Jumbletop, Battles."

" Oh, yes, Battles. I'm sure you deserve this pretty book, and that it—(m. m. m. er. m.)

In your Scripture paper, Coxey, you say that you renounce the devil and all his works; but when asked what was meant by the devil's works, you say—er—his insides.

Looking over the mathematical papers, I notice that Edward Shirker has placed at the end of his paper, " No time to finish." As he has only attempted one question, and the attempt is a poor one, the above statement requires some explanation. James Mucker has left on record that two sides of a triangle are equal to the third—which I find—ah—difficult to credit. Also that the diameter of anything is when it's cut in two—another somewhat elusive statement. The prize for mathematics goes to Oliver Omelet, his only mistake being, I believe, a clerical one; parallel lines, my dear Oliver, meet at infinity—not divinity. Your prize is entitled: " How to extract the Cube Root," a New and Painless Method, by Silas Guff.

Lady Jumbletop; I have no doubt—(m. hm. ah.

h'm.) Master (insert reciter's name) has not given
any indication of intelligence in any branch of learning. However, in the General Knowledge paper he
has defined a demagogue as a large vessel generally
filled with whiskey. As this seems to contain a partial
truth, I have given him half a mark, and the prize
for general improvement.

The Natural History class has, at last, learnt the
difference between wild and tame ducks, and ascer-
tained that a farmer's dog's bite is worse than his
bark. Binks minor acquired the knowledge—in ex-
change for his little finger—that unloaded guns go
off more frequently than the loaded variety.

However, there has been a distinct advance on
the work of last term, when you may remember my
young friend William Muffins mistook a hornet's nest
for a football, and tried to punt it over the orchard,
with somewhat—er—painful results. This prize is
awarded to Binks minor. As you have not got your
glasses, Lady Jumbletop, may I read the name of
the book?

    "Straight Talks with a Snail."

   By the Author of " Glimpses of Goose Life."

   Lady Jumbletop: I'm sure you enjoy—(m. m. er.
m.)

The prize in the Nature Study class goes to Henry
Halfbake. The prize volume is entitled:

       " Habits of the Sloth."

   By the Author of " The Slug's Progress."

In the Chemistry and Physical Research class, I
note with pleasure that there have been fewer attempts
to destroy the assistant. Nitro-glycerine, my dear

Halfbake, does not remove the spots from clothes; it removes—er—the clothes.   James Daftie, who was given a sample of prussic acid to analyse, and mistook the reaction for ginger-beer, is fortunately still among us.   The prize in the chemistry class has been awarded to George Muddler:

"Molecules I have Met."

Ode to Spring.

By the Author of "What a Germ Should Know."

And now, before we part to our several homes, we should thank Lady Jumbletop for the kind way in which she has distributed the prizes this afternoon. I propose three cheers for Lady Jumbletop.   Now, Larksmeadians, all together!

(Three cheers for the Head!)

Boys! I thank you.   And now dear lady, I'm sure you're dying for a cup of tea.

Three cheers for the holidays, boys! . . . .

I think we may leave them to themselves now.